MILITARY AIRCRAFT ON DISPLAY
FIRST WORLD WAR TO THE PRESENT DAY

Royston Morris

AMBERLEY

First published 2025

Amberley Publishing
The Hill, Stroud,
Gloucestershire, GL5 4EP

www.amberley-books.com

ISBN: 978 1 3981 2379 3 (print)
ISBN: 978 1 3981 2380 9 (ebook)

British Library Cataloguing in Publication Data.
A catalogue record for this book is available from the British Library.

Typeset in 9pt on 12pt Celeste.
Typesetting by Hurix Digital, India.
Printed in the UK.

Appointed GPSR EU Representative: Easy Access System Europe Oü, 16879218
Address: Mustamäe tee 50, 10621, Tallinn, Estonia
Contact Details: gpsr.requests@easproject.com, +358 40 500 3575

Contents

Acknowledgements

The author would like to thank the following, for granting permission to allow photographs taken at their premises to be published in this book. The abbreviated forms are used throughout the book.

London Science Museum (LSM), South Kensington www.sciencemuseum.org.uk

Royal Air Force Museum (RAFM), London (RAFH), Cosford (RAFC)
www.rafmuseum.org.uk

Imperial War Museum (IWM), Duxford (IWMD), Lambeth (IWML)
www.iwm.org.uk

The Helicopter Museum (HCM), Weston-super-Mare
www.helimuseum.com

National Museum of The Royal Navy – Fleet Air Arm Museum (FAAM), Yeovilton
www.nmrm.org.uk

Cavan & Leitrim Railway Museum (C&LR), Dromod
www.cavanandleitrimrailway.com

Dumfries & Galloway Aviation Museum (D&GM), Dumfries
www.dumfriesaviationmuseum.com

National Museum of Flight – Scotland (NMFS), East Fortune
www.nms.ac.uk

The Museum of Army Flying (MAF), Middle Wallop
www.armyflying.com

Aerospace Bristol, Filton
www.aerospace.org

North East Land, Sea & Air Museum (NELSAM), Sunderland
www.nelsam.org.uk

Gatwick Aviation Museum (GAMC), Charlwood
www.gamc.org.uk

Midland Air Museum (MAM), Baginton
www.midlandairmuseum.co.uk

Brooklands Aviation & Motoring Museum (BAMM), Weybridge
www.brooklandsmuseum.com

Bournemouth Aviation Museum (BAM), Christchurch
www.bamhurn.org

South Yorkshire Aircraft Museum (SYAM), Doncaster
www.southyorkshireaircraftmuseum.org.uk

Caernarfon Airworld Aviation Museum (CAAM), Llandwrog
www.airworldmuseum.com

Cornwall at War Museum (CWM), Davidstow
www.cornwallatwarmuseum.co.uk

Boscombe Down Aviation Collection (BDAC), Old Sarum
www.boscombedownaviationcollection.co.uk

Farnborough Air Sciences Trust Museum (FAST), Farnborough
www.airsciences.org.uk

Berkshire Aviation Museum (BkAM), Woodley
www.museumofberkshireaviation.co.uk

Ulster Folk & Transport Museum (UFT), Cultra
www.ulsterfolkmuseum.org

Abbreviations

A+AEE	Aeroplane & Armament Experimental Establishment, Boscombe Down
AAC	Army Air Cadets
AFC	Army Flying Corps
AHB	Air Historical Branch
ATC	Air Training Corps
FAA	Fleet Air Arm
MU	Maintenance Unit
RAAF	Royal Australian Air Force
RAE	Royal Aircraft Establishment – General
RAEB/F	Royal Aircraft Establishment, Boscombe Down/Farnborough
RAF	Royal Air Force
RCAF	Royal Canadian Air Force
RFC	Royal Flying Corps
RIAT	Royal International Air Tattoo
RN	Royal Navy
RNAS	Royal Naval Air Station
USAAF	United States Army Air Force
USAF	United States Air Force
USMC	United States Marine Corps
USN	United States Navy

Introduction

On 17 December 1903 the Wright brothers made the first ever controlled sustained powered flight, flying a distance of 852 feet in Kill Devil Hills, North Carolina, with Wilbur at the controls. They were not, however, the first men to fly – that honour goes to balloonists Jean-Francois Pilatre de Rozier and Francois d'Arlandes in 1783, who travelled a distance of 5.59 miles in their Montgolfier hot air balloon.

By the First World War aircraft design had moved on, with craft being fitted with more powerful engines. Biplanes began to take over from monoplanes, with significant numbers being commissioned by various air forces. Aircraft development gained in momentum and in the late 1930s, with the uncertainty of the threat from Hitler looming large, jet fighters and bombers were being manufactured in sizeable numbers for RAF and significant Allied forces within Europe. When an aircraft begins service in a military capacity it is taken on charge (TOC), and struck off charge (SOC) at the end of its military career.

With the end of the Second World War came a new threat. When the alliance between the Americans and the Russians grew strained, both sides began supporting opposing sides in conflicts known as proxy wars, and these sides became known as the Eastern and Western Blocs. This tension was referred to as the Cold War because neither of the two superpowers were involved in major large-scale fighting with each other. This war ended with the disbandment of the Soviet Union in 1991, but during the period 1946 to 1991, both nations had significantly increased aircraft numbers.

Following the Cold War, there was a period termed as 'Cold War II', again with neither superpower being directly involved in large-scale conflict, but both having differing opinions in wars that have happened since 1991 – such as the Gulf and Afghanistan wars, the recurring Arab-Israeli conflict that rears its ugly head every so often. With Russia being heavily involved in a war against Ukraine, tensions and relationships have become increasingly strained. Also with the uncertainty surrounding North Korea, both superpowers and their respective allies are prepared, alert and ready should things ever come to a head, ending up in what could potentially be World War III.

Chapter One

First World War, 1914–18

On 28 June 1914 the heir to the Austro-Hungarian throne, Archduke Franz Ferdinand, was assassinated by a Bosnian Serb. Austria-Hungary held Serbia responsible and on 28 July 1914 they began a war against them, which would last for just over four years and would eventually involve the Russians, Germans, French, British and the Ottoman Empire.

The first planes used in combat against each other occurred on 1 July 1915 involving a German Fokker and a French Morane-Saulnier plane, the German craft coming out the victor by shooting the French plane down. Although the first ever built military biplane was by the Wright brothers in 1909, it wasn't until early 1916 that they really started being produced in significant numbers by various manufacturers and used in combat throughout the First World War.

The Dutch-built Fokker E.111 Eindecker monoplane was the first aircraft with synchronization gear and could fire the 7.92-mm machine gun through the arc of the propeller without hitting the blades.

This 1916 example, serial number 210/16, the only survivor out of 249, was brought down the same year in the Somme area, and was taken to the War Office for evaluation. Donated to LSM in 1918, it is seen on 22 February 2020 – minus fabric covering to illustrate its internal construction.

The Caudron G.3 reconnaissance sesquiplane (biplane with the upper wing much longer than the lower one). This 1916 example could carry a single light machine gun and hand-released bombs, TOC with Belgian Air Force. SOC in 1921, it was a civilian aircraft until privately purchased in 1936. Acquired by RAFM in 1964, it is seen on 5 January 2024 at RAFH.

Royal Aircraft Factory (RAirF) built numerous aircraft for the RAF, but some craft were subcontracted out and built under licence.

This 1916 Ruston, Proctor & Co.-built BE.2c biplane was TOC with RFC, and later with various RAF squadrons on night training exercises. During 1918 it crashed in unknown circumstances. SOC in May 1919 and donated to IWML in September. In 2012 it was transported to the IWMD. It is pictured on 23 September 2023.

Sopwith Aviation Co. built the 'Scout' single-seater fighter biplane – given the nickname 'Pup' by pilots. This nickname set the precedent that all later planes built by the company (except triplanes) were given animal names – earning them the monicker 'The Flying Zoo Creators'.

This example was built in 1916, TOC with RNAS, flew in the Western Front during the conflict, and SOC in 1921. Recovered from France in 1960, it was extensively rebuilt by RAFC. It is seen on 23 December 2023.

The Bristol F.2B First World War fighter and reconnaissance biplane was used by RFC, Polish and Honduran air forces. Built by British & Colonial Aeroplane Co., this example was built in 1917, TOC with RFC, and in 1918 transferred to RAF Home Defence Squadron. Its last flight was in 1920, SOC, coming under the ownership of IWMD in 1922. It is pictured on 23 September 2023.

Sopwith subcontracted out the manufacturing of some of their triplanes. This example, seen at RAFH on 5 January 2024, was built by Oakley & Co. Ltd in late 1917. One of only two out of 147 built that survive, there are several replicas. It never saw combat action, serving with the School of Aerial Fighting & Gunnery. After the First World War it was displayed in a temporary exhibition at IWM until 1924. Found languishing in Cardington dump, it was rescued by RAF in 1936, almost lost again in 1945, rescued, restored, and on display in 1964.

'Dreidecker' translates to triplane, and Fokker manufactured the 'DR.1' for Imperial German Air Service. This type was made famous by ace pilot Baron Manfred Albrecht Freiherr Von Richthofen (aka 'The Red Baron'), reporting to his Commander-General that they were superior to the Sopwith and all fighter squadrons should have them.

This example (only known survivor out of 320), serial number 528/17, built in 1917, was retained after the First World War as a testbed by German Aviation Research Institute, and crashed in unknown circumstances during the 1930s. Displayed in an 'as found' condition at Capel Military Show, Surrey, on 2 July 2022.

Richard Garrett & Sons built this FE.2b under licence on behalf of the RairF. in 1917. For some reason the main fuselage wasn't constructed as a plane and it languished unfinished in the factory. Acquired at an auction of surplus items in 1933, in 1976 it was donated to RAFM, remaining in store until 1987. Reproduction parts were manufactured to complete the aircraft. The restoration rebuild was finished in 2008, and it is seen on 5 January 2024 suspended from the ceiling at RAFH.

In 1918 Wolseley Motors Ltd built this SE.5A biplane single-seater fighter under licence for the RAirF. TOC with RAF, it was sent directly to the Western Front. SOC in 1924, civilian registration G-EBIC, it was one of thirty-five sold to Savage Skywriting Co. In 1936 it was acquired by International Horseless Carriage Corporation, and its civilian registration was cancelled in 1938. Stored at Brooklands during the Second World War, in 1950 it moved to 39 MU Colerne for restoration, followed by years taking part in air displays until 1959, when it moved to 71 MU at Heathrow for further restoration. Donated to RAFM in 1992 and in store until 2003, it moved to RAFH and is pictured on 5 January 2024.

This DH.9A bomber, built in 1918 by Westland Aircraft, was involved in bombing missions over German cities Frankfurt, Cologne, Koblenz and Kaiserslautern. On 5 October 1918 it was forced into making a crash landing and the crew were captured and released after armistice.

In 1936 it was on display with over 100 other craft at Berlin Air Museum. In 1943 the museum was heavily damaged by fire following an RAF bombing raid, destroying almost all of its craft. In 1967 remains were discovered in store at Krakow, Poland. Negotiations began and in 1977 it was exchanged for a Spitfire. Restoration was completed in 1983 and it is seen at RAFH on 5 January 2024.

Deemed superior to SE.5s and Sopwith Camels, the Fokker D.VII fighter biplane was made from welded steel-tubed frames produced en masse using techniques pioneered by the American automotive industry. Herman Goering was a D.VII fighter pilot ace before becoming Hitler's head of Luftwaffe. Such a feared aircraft, the 1919 Armistice Treaty of Versailles mentions it by name as the only item of equipment to have its entire stock passed to the victors.

This 1918-built example was left in Ostend by retreating Germans. TOC with Belgian Air Force until 1931, SOC and purchased by a collector in 1937. Ownership then passed to RAFM in 1966. On 5 January 2024 it was suspended from the ceiling at RAFH.

RAirF built the RE.8 reconnaissance and bomber biplane, which was used by RFC and RAF during the First World War. 4,077 were built but only two survive.

This 1918 example, built under licence by Daimler, arrived in France on Armistice Day, in its packing crate. As hostilities had ceased it was returned to RAF Tadcaster. Retrieved from RAF Cardington's scrap line in 1935, it was sent to IWML and suspended from the ceiling, but was damaged in 1943 when the building was hit by a bomb. RAF carried out repairs on the craft, completed in 1949, and it returned to Lambeth until 1974. Sent to IWMD for display, it is seen on 23 September 2023.

Sopwith produced the Dolphin 5F.1 fighter planes during 1918/1919. The type was deemed obsolete in 1921. This 1918 example was TOC as part of the home defence until early 1919. Its post-First World War history is unknown to the author. In June 1967 an advert for 'old plane parts' was placed in Exchange & Mart, and these parts (including the front fuselage) were purchased by RAFM. Restoration work began in 1973, although it was suspended in 1974 due to workshops moving. The craft was recorded in 1989 as being a 'box of parts'. The rear fuselage was purchased from Kent Arms Sales in 1989 and restoration recommenced in 1997. Completed in 2012, it was sent to RAFH and is seen on 5 January 2024.

Sopwith Camels were built by Sopwith Aviation Co. and various sub-contractors. William & Beardmore of Glasgow built this shipboard variant Camel 2F.1 in 1918. Gaining notoriety on 11 August that year, the pilot ascended to a height of 19,000 feet and attacked and shot down the Imperial German Navy's flagship rigid Zeppelin bomber airship LZ 100. Acquired by IWML in 1920, it travelled to different locations throughout the country, returning to IWML in 2014. Seen on 4 November 2016.

Vickers Ltd built the Vimy IV maritime patrol heavy bomber biplane for the RAF. TOC in 1918, it saw action on the Western Front until Armistice Day. It then returned to Vickers, SOC, and modified to enable John Alcock & Arthur Brown to make the first transatlantic crossing in 1919 – taking 15 hours and 57 minutes. Acquired by LSM in 1920, it is seen 100 years later on 22 February 2020.

Chapter Two

The Interwar Years, 1919–38

During this period there was a huge upsurge in demand by businesses to have planes built to carry their customers and airline companies increased in number. The demand for passenger planes was gaining in momentum.

There were military aircraft built during this period, but they were limited in number as there was no real threat or fear of any conflict on the horizon. This, however, all changed in 1934 when Adolf Hitler declared himself the 'Fuhrer (leader) of all Germany' and thus began his years of dictatorship, corruption, power and torture, resulting in the deaths of millions of people.

Built in 1930 at Filton as a demonstration fighter for the RAF, this Bulldog 105 MkIIa was used for demonstration and development purposes, participating in various air shows. In 1938 it was on temporary display at LSM until the outbreak of the Second World War, when it was stored at Wapping. In 1955 it was loaned to Pinewood Studios for the Douglas Bader film *Reach for the Sky.*

Returned to Filton in 1957, it was restored to flying condition, which was completed in 1961. In 1964 at Farnborough Air Show it crashed doing a loop-de-loop manoeuvre and was declared a write-off. The following year RAFM recovered the wreckage from the scrap dump at Farnborough. It remained in storage for twenty-nine years until 1994 when restoration began, which was completed 1999, In March that year it was taken to RAFH and is pictured on 5 January 2024.

The Nimrod carrier-based fighter biplane was built by Hawker Aircraft Ltd for use with FAA. This example (seen at IWMD on 23 September 2023), MkI, built in 1932, was the third one off the production line. TOC with RN on board HMS *Glorious*, serial number S1581, it was used until 10 February 1938 when it crashed at Hal Far in Malta and SOC.

In 1970 remains were salvaged from a scrapyard in London, which were donated to RAFM, where it remained in store until 1994, then sent to Aero-Vintage for restoration, completed in April 2000. Three months later it made its first post-restoration flight from Henlow to Jersey. In August 2002 it was transferred to Fighter Collection at IWMD.

Built by Stearman Aircraft Corporation in the 1930s/40s, the PT-17 Model 95 Kaydet trainer biplane was used by USAF. This 1933 example is pictured in the American Air Museum at IWMD on 23 September 2023. Following the end of the Second World War, it was sold to a private company as a crop sprayer. Having changed owners about four times since 1952, it was donated to IWM in 1973.

The Cierva C30A autogyro was designed by Juan De La Cierva and built under licence, with seventy-eight being constructed by A.V. Roe & Co. They were classified by RAF as 'Rota 671', as light observational and radar calibration craft. There are eleven survivors – four in the UK.

Serial number K4232 was built in 1934 and TOC with RAF at Old Sarum. It served with various RAF squadrons for the next twelve years. SOC in 1946, it was sold to a Swedish company for training purposes. In 1967 it was put into storage in Sweden until 1977, then acquired by RAFM and restored, completed in 1980. It is seen at RAFH on 5 January 2024.

This 1935 Cierva C-30A as G-ACWM was sold to the Autogiro Flying Club. In June 1940 it was seconded into military service at Duxford, retaining its civilian registration until September and given serial number AP 506. TOC with RAF in February 1941, it served until 1945, then was put into storage at Kemble. Remaining until April 1946, SOC and up for disposal, it was acquired and re-registered to its original number, then sold again in 1948 and in storage between 1949 and 1953. By 1964 it had moved to Staverton Airport, where it sustained fire damage and was transported to Tewkesbury. In 1983 it was discovered in pieces in a barn near Tewkesbury and acquired. In 1988 it was donated to HCM and put on display in an 'as found unrestored' condition. Seen on 28 September 2023.

The Hawker 'Fury' fast agile fighter biplane, the first interceptor used by the RAF, was capable of speeds of up to 200 mph. This 1935 example (serial number K5674) was the only surviving airworthy one out of 275. TOC with RAF, it served until 1940, SOC, then shipped to Durban, South Africa. TOC with South African Air Force until 1941, it made a forced landing due to running out of fuel, after which it was recorded as SOC and scrapped in 1943.

In 1992 remains were discovered in a barn in South Africa, which were recovered back to the UK for restoration in 1994. In 2003 restoration was complete, and it was given the civilian registration G-CBZP. It made its first post-restoration flight in 2012 based at IWMD, and it is pictured here on 23 September 2023.

Built in 1930, this Hawker Hart II was one of four built as civilian demonstration aircraft. Registered as G-ABMR, it took part in the 1932 Hendon Air Display. Between 1931 and 1936 it was used as a test bed for Rolls-Royce Kestrel engines. In August 1939 Hawker Engineering at Brooklands bought it and in early 1940 it was registered J9941. TOC with RAF as a light bomber and photographic reconnaissance craft until November 1946, its final permit to fly expired and it was SOC. Between 1949 and 1971 it was on static display at various locations and flew in several air displays, then withdrawn from flying. In 1972 it was taken to RAFH, and is pictured on 5 January 2024.

K8042 was a 'Gladiator' fighting biplane ordered from Gloster Aircraft Ltd in 1935, the last of the fighter biplanes used by the RAF. TOC from new in 1937 at Kemble, by 1941 it was a testing unit to trial out various machine guns. Used extensively through the war with various RAF fighting units, in 1946 it was deemed 'obsolete from flying' and for 'display purposes only' and SOC. Between 1954 and 1965 it was in storage most of the time, but was on display at the 1960 Battle of Britain week celebrations. Refurbished in 1967 at RAF Henlow, the following year it took part in the RAF's 50th Anniversary Royal Review & Battle of Britain week again. In 1971 it was moved from Henlow to RAFH, then moved to RAFC in November 2016. It is seen on 23 December 2023.

Military serial number K4672 was one of eight Hawker Hind light bombers ordered in 1937 by the newly formed Royal Afghan Air Force. It was delivered in crates to Kabul airfield, arriving December that year and TOC. This example was in service until 1967 and SOC. In 1968 it was acquired by RAFM and taken to RAFC. It is pictured on 23 December 2023.

A Miles M.14 Magister twin-seat monoplane RAF aircrew trainer. During training the pilot would occupy the front seat and the trainee would be in the rear. This example (an MkA type) was built under licence by Phillips & Powis in 1937, TOC with RAF in Woodley, serial number BB 661, and served until SOC in 1963, then civilian registered G-AFBS. Acquired by IWMD in 1978, it is pictured on 23 September 2023. Note: the 'blind-flying hood' behind the second seat covered the trainee's head in flight during training to enable them to use the controls during flight in black-out conditions. The instructions were relayed via an inbuilt microphone from the pilot.

The Avro Anson multi-purpose aircraft was developed in the mid-1930s and saw service with RAF, FAA, RCAF and RAAF during and after the Second World War.

This MkI example (serial number N6877), pictured at IWMD on 23 September 2023, was built in 1938 and TOC with RAF. SOC in 1950, civilian registration G-AMDA, it was used by Elstree studios for filming purposes. Involved in a minor accident in November 1972, it was put into storage and its civilian registration was cancelled in 1981. Arriving at IWMD in 1988, it was restored to its original form.

Boulton & Paul Ltd began aircraft manufacturing in 1915. The Defiant turret-fighter/interceptor jet could concentrate their firepower on enemy bombers. It had a four-gun turret behind the main cockpit. 1,064 were built but this 1938 example is the only complete survivor.

TOC with RAF, it served with ten different squadrons. SOC after thirty years' service, it was preserved at RAFH in 1971. In 2009 it was sent to Rochester Airport and restored to its former glory by Medway Aircraft Preservation Society. Completed in 2012, it was returned to RAFH, then in 2016 transported to RAFC, where it is seen on 23 December 2023.

The Hawker Hurricane single-seater jet fighter was an icon during the Second World War. Taking part in the Battle of Britain, it was overshadowed by the Spitfire in the public eye, but in reality Hurricanes inflicted 70 per cent of losses incurred by the Luftwaffe during that conflict.

Serial number L1592 was built in 1938 and TOC with RAF. In August 1940 it was attacked by Messerschmitt Bf-109E and forced into crash landing, sustaining minor damage. It was taken to RAF Henlow for repair and returned to service. In 1945 it was transferred to RAF Sealand, SOC and stored for future museum use. In 1950 it was allocated to AHB travelling exhibit until 1954, then stored at RAF Sydenham. In 1960 it was transported to Dunsford and restored to static display standards. In May 1961 it was owned by LSM. It is pictured on 22 February 2020.

Chapter Three

Second World War, 1939–45

On 1 September 1939 the Western World changed forever when Hitler's Nazi Germany invaded Poland. Two days later Britain and France declared war on Germany, after they had failed to cease military operations – and thus began a war which would last for a day over six years. This conflict would eventually involve Japan, China, Russia, Denmark, Norway, North Africa, Canada and America, to name a few. It was also the war which resulted in the most deaths of any other in human history – with an estimated 50 to 85 million people losing their lives.

The design of military aircraft during this period had advanced and escalated on a grand scale, with Jet Fighters and Heavy Duty Bombers being manufactured in vast numbers by the British, German, Russian and American forces. Companies expanded their factories and workforces in order to meet the ever-increasing demand for different types of aircraft from various governments.

No book about military aircraft would be complete without including the iconic single-seater fighter Supermarine Spitfire. K9942 was the 155th built, in April 1939, and the oldest surviving one in existence. TOC with RAF at Church Fenton, it flew thirty-two operational sorties including in the Battle of Britain.

Involved in an accident in 1943, it was placed in storage in 1944 and SOC – and never flew again. After the war it appeared in two films: the 1952 *Angels One Five* and 1969 *Battle of Britain*. Continuing on public display at numerous events, in 1971 it was owned by RAFM and noted on 23 December 2023 at RAFC.

Halifax Heavy Bombers were fitted with nine .303-inch machine guns and could carry a 13,000-lb payload. This 1942 example, serial number W1048, was built by English Electric and TOC with RAF. In April 1942 it took off with ten others from RAF Kinloss to Norway to attack German battleship *Tirpitz*. The eighth aircraft to attack at 00.30 a.m., it flew at a mere 200 feet to release its bombs – a success – only to be hit by flak from the *Tirpitz*, suffering extensive damage. The pilot, realising the damage was too severe to make it to neutral Sweden, made a perfect wheels-up landing on the frozen surface of Lake Hoklingen, 25 miles from Trondheim. The crew escaped and were taken prisoner; twelve hours later, the craft sank into 92 feet of water. In 1971 it was found by local divers, and in 1973 successfully lifted from its watery grave by RAF Sub Aqua Club and returned to the UK. On 5 January 2024 it is seen at RAFH in an 'unrestored as found' condition.

Westland Lysander co-operation and liaison aircraft. This 1940-built MkIII (serial number 99125) was TOC with RAF in reconnaissance patrols over Hampshire and the Isle of Wight. In September 1941 it was returned to Westland and modified for target towing duties. It served with several RAF units including Special Duties Squadron, working alongside French resistance, responsible for transporting 'secret agents' to and from France. In 1946 Lysanders were declared obsolete by the RAF and SOC. This example was transferred to RAF Stanmore Park into deep storage. In 1958 it started being put on static display at various military tattoos, RAF open days and air shows, and in 1971 it moved to RAFH. It is seen on 5 January 2024.

Yokosuka MXY-7 Ohka Model 11 jet-powered suicide aircraft were flown surprisingly by volunteer members of Imperial Japanese Navy Air Service Special Attack Units termed as 'Kamikaze' flights. These pilots were prepared to die for their emperor, country, family and honour, with average ages between seventeen and nineteen years old, and given seven days of training to prepare them. Over 750 were built by Naval Air Arsenal in Japan during 1944/45. Only about 10 per cent of missions were successful, destroying over fifty Allied ships. Pilots were allowed to return if targets could not be located or their craft developed a malfunction – many did return only to be executed for cowardice. These craft had a 23-mile range and were loaded with a 2,600-lb warhead. This example, seen at IWML on 15 June 2024, was one of several brought back from the Far East after hostilities ended.

N1854, a Fairey Aviation Co. Fulmar carrier-borne British reconnaissance/fighter plane, was built in 1940, TOC with FAA, and served until July 1946, seeing plenty of action in various conflicts during the war. After the hostilities and SOC, it returned to Fairey to be re-registered with civilian number G-AIBE. In 1951 it was on display at RAFH for a public open day, and in April 1959 it went to Silloth. Its original military markings were reapplied for the film *Sinking of The Ark Royal*. In 1962 it was acquired by FAAM and in 1971 flew from Yeovilton to Scotland while taking part in an RNAS Open Day at Lossiemouth. It was on display at Yeovilton on 16 December 2023.

The Fiat CR.42 Falco was the last single-seat fighter sesquiplane to be manufactured by any Second World War combatant. They took part in the Battle of Britain, but were totally outclassed by RAF fighters, suffering many losses, leading to limited usage in the conflict. This 1940 example, TOC with Royal Italian Air Force, had the serial number MM5701. On 11 November 1940 on a raid from Belgium to Harwich, it was forced to land on a beach in Orfordness and tipped over onto its nose. The pilot was taken prisoner, and the plane was later repaired and restored by the RAF, TOC with them (serial number BT 474) and used for flight trials. Between April 1941 and October 1942 it was used to develop front-line tactics in the form of mock combats. Followed by many years of storage at various RAF locations, SOC in 1978, it was acquired by RAFM, then moved to RAFH. It is seen on 5 January 2024.

The Messerschmitt Bf109 was the backbone of the Luftwaffe's fighter force, built by Bayerische Flugzeugwerke Messerschmitt. This April 1940-built example took part in and survived dogfights during the early stages of the Battle of Britain, but its military career was short-lived, coming to an end on 30 September that year. An inexperienced twenty-two-year-old pilot should have been part of the escort on a bombing raid over London, but missed the rendezvous with the bombers after being intercepted by Spitfires over Beachy Head. Forced to land at East Dean, the pilot climbed out of the cockpit and was shot in the hand and jaw by an over-enthusiastic Home Guard member and taken prisoner. The plane was recovered and toured around America and Canada, returning to the UK in 1943 and taken to RAF Hurn for storage. Donated to IWMD, it is on display in a recreation of its crash landing. Pictured on 23 September 2023.

Fairey Aviation Co. built the Albacore single-engine biplane torpedo bombers. N4172 was built in October 1940 and TOC with RN FAA. 1 April 1941 was nothing to laugh about for the pilot and crew; during a blizzard in A'Mhoine, Whitten Head, Sutherland, they made an emergency crash landing. N4172 miraculously remained where it crashed for over thirty-three years until October 1974, when the wreckage was recovered and taken to RAF Kinloss, then Wroughton for storage. Later it was taken to Land's End Airfield as a project rebuild for FAAM (completed in 1987). On 5 September 2019 it was pictured inside the museum's reserve collection in Cobham Hall. It is the only complete surviving example out of 800. Note how the wings fold back alongside the fuselage when the craft is not in use.

A.V. Roe manufactured another icon of the Second World War – the four-engined heavy bomber Lancaster, which could carry the heaviest bombs of the RAF (22,000 lb). The stalwarts of night bombing raids over Germany, over 608,612 tons of incendiaries were dropped in 156,000 sorties. Seen on 5 January 2024 at RAFH, this 1942 example, ordered as a twin-engined Manchester bomber but completed as a Lancaster B.1, TOC with the RAF and serial number R5868, took part in sixty-eight bombing sorties between June 1942 and March 1943. During the latter date it collided with another Lancaster at 20,000 feet on a raid over Berlin, limping home to England. It was repaired and returned to service the following April. In August 1945 it was declared as a museum piece and transferred into storage. Two years later it was deemed as non-effective stock. Serial number 7325M, SOC in 1956, was transferred to AHB at Wroughton, and by 1958 it had been dismantled and put into storage at RAF Fulbeck until 1970, when it was moved to Army Workshops, Bicester, rebuilt and restored, before going to RAFH in 1972.

The Lockheed Hudson light bomber and coastal reconnaissance plane was built by Lockheed Aircraft Corporation. This example at RAFH on 5 January 2024 was built in 1942 for the RAF, but before it was delivered it was shipped to Laverton, Western Australia. TOC with RAAF, it was involved in an extensive series of raids on Japanese shipping and ground positions. It suffered port (left) side engine failure on numerous occasions and SOC in 1946.

In 1947 Macquarie Grove Flying School purchased it for a measly £150 (Hudson's sold for £500). In 1950 it was acquired by *Sydney Morning Herald Newspaper* to air-drop papers to remote country areas. Withdrawn from service in May 1952, it was removed from the civilian register, but re-introduced back in October 1954, changing ownership with half a dozen companies, for aerial survey/photography work. In July 1981 it was auctioned by Christies and sold to RAFM for £16,000, arriving at RAFH in January 1982.

At 07.48 a.m. (Hawaiian time) on 7 December 1941 over 350 Japanese aircraft took off from six aircraft carriers in the Pacific Ocean and attacked the neutral USA fleet based at Pearl Harbor, destroying 180 aircraft, sinking twelve ships and causing 2,403 American deaths. America declared war against Japan the next day.

USAAF fighters/bombers were sent to attack Japanese fleets. The first dispatched were Curtiss-Wright P-40 Warhawk fighter-bombers. This 1942 example, TOC with USAAF, serial number A29-556, was one of fifty due to be sent to the Pacific – this somehow never happened. In 1943 it was shipped to Australia. In May 1944 it was damaged in a landing accident after being struck by another craft and SOC by September, written off to 'components only'. In 1974 its main fuselage, with five other crash site wrecks, was shipped to California, painstakingly restored and formed into this composite craft. In 2003 it was donated to RAFH, and noted on 5 January 2024.

FW190 single-engine German fighters were built by Focke-Wulf Flugzeugbau and used by the Luftwaffe. This 1943 example (pictured on 23 December 2023 at RAFC) was part of a 'Mistel'.

The 'Mistel' involved a small piloted craft attached to the back of a larger unmanned craft – the larger craft was under the complete control of the piloted craft and fitted with a 8,380-lb warhead. The ensemble would fly to the designated target area, release the warhead to do its damage and head home to reload another warhead.

This FW190 was captured (with its JU88 'Mistel') in Tirstrup, Denmark, in June 1945. The following month the whole ensemble was ferried to Schleswig, Germany – JU 88 was scrapped. Delivered to Farnborough, it was used for testing purposes. Between 1946 and 1960 it was on display at RAF Cranwell, then taken into storage until 1964, arriving at IWML until December 2012, when it was transferred to RAFC.

Junkers Flugzeug-und Motorenwerke AG built the most important craft used by the Luftwaffe – the Junkers JU88 twin-engined multi-purpose fighter/bomber. This early 1943 example was TOC with the Luftwaffe, serial number D5 + EV. By May that year it was flown to RAF Dyce by a defecting German pilot. Within five days of arriving in Scotland, it was flown to RAEF, then to RAF Collyweston in May 1944, until 1946, when it was transferred to AHB. Between then and 1973 it spent time at half a dozen AHB locations. Restored during 1974/75, it was on display at RAFH from 1976 to February 2017, before being moved to RAFC. Seen on 23 December 2023.

This American four-engined Boeing B-17 Flying Fortress bomber, serial number 44-85784, was built in 1944 by Lockheed-Vega and TOC with USAAF. In 1950 it was loaned to General Electric Flight Test Center at Schenectady for infra-red tracking trials. SOC in 1954, it was sent for disposal at Olmsted Air Force Base, then acquired by National Geographic Institute in Paris, civilian registration F-BGSR, remaining there for twenty years. In 1975 it was sold to Euroworld Ltd at Biggin Hill, registered N17TE, taking part at various air shows throughout UK. In 1982 it appeared in London Weekend Television series *We'll Meet Again*. In 1985 it was given a certificate of airworthiness and civilian registration G-BEDF. Then in 1990 it was used in the film *Memphis Belle*. In 2000 it transferred to B17 Preservation Ltd based at Duxford airfield (pictured on 23 September 2023).

In 1944 at Willow Run, Michigan, Ford Motor Company built, under licence to Consolidated Aircraft Corporation, this B-24 Liberator heavy bomber. TOC with USAAF, serial number 44-50206, and SOC in June 1945, it was immediately TOC with the RAF (serial number KN 751) for the closing stages of the war, based on Cocos Islands in the Indian Ocean, taking part in bombing missions over Japanese-owned Dutch East Indies and dropping supplies to Allied guerrillas in Malaya. SOC and transferred to Bengal later that year, it was placed in open storage in 1946. In April 1947 TOC with Indian Air Force (as HE 807) until December 1968, it was then moved into storage at Poona. In 1974 it arrived at RAF Lyneham, SOC, and acquired by RAFM. In 1976 it was on display at RAFC until 2005, when it was moved by road to RAFH. Noted on 5 January 2024.

Two-seater dive bomber/attack aircraft JU-87 was built by Junkers. In 1944 this 87G-2 Stuka variant left the factory in Dessau and became Luftwaffe serial number RI+JK. In May 1945 it was captured by British forces in northern Germany and assigned serial number 8474M. Between September 1945 and March 1967 it moved around various RAF locations as a static display at air shows. In 1969 it was used in the filming of the *Battle of Britain*, then transferred to AHB at St Athan. In 1970 it moved to RAF Colerne for temporary display. In 1978 it moved permanently to RAFH. It was noted on 5 January 2024. Note the tank motif on the nose cone, which were the main targets for these aircraft.

Mitsubishi Aircraft Co. built the Ki-46 twin-engined reconnaissance aircraft for the Imperial Japanese Army Air Force. This 1944 example, built at Nagoya, was one of the Ki-46-IIIs allocated to 81 Sentai (Group), part of 3 Chutai (Squadron). In August 1945 the Japanese surrendered, and in September the Commander of Kahan Airfield in Malaya was ordered to hand over the two of these craft being used. In early 1946 they were made airworthy and flown to Singapore for shipping to England. The 'Rising Sun' discs were replaced with RAF roundels. They became part of AHB in late 1955. A period of eight years in storage at various locations followed, until they were put on display at RAF Biggin Hill in 1963. Another eight years of storage followed, after which they were on display at the 'Battle of Britain' show in 1971 at RAF St Athan. After restoration this example took part in the 1982 'Battle of Britain' display. In 1998 the MoD donated the craft to RAFC, and it later transferred to RAFH. Seen on 5 January 2024.

The P-51 Mustang long-range single-seater fighter/fighter-bomber served with USAAF, RAF, RCAF and others for forty-four years. In 1944 this example left North American Aviation factory, TOC with USAAF, serial number 44-73979, serving until 1950. TOC with RCAF, serial number 9246, it served until SOC in 1960, becoming a gate guardian at RCAF Saint Jean in Quebec. It remained there for eight years, before it was acquired by IWMD, remaining until 1989. Moved to IWML where it was suspended from the ceiling (seen on 20 April 2013), by September 2014 it had returned to IWMD.

British-built Vickers-Armstrong Ltd long-range medium bomber the 'Wellington'. This 1944 Blackpool-built version (seen at RAFC on 23 December 2023), a B.MkX version, was TOC with RAF. In 1948 Boulton Paul removed the front turret, replacing it with a fairing and fitted-out interior with navigation training equipment. 270 Wellingtons were treated the same way, converting them to T.MkX.

In 1949 it was used for navigation training and practice bombing over ranges. In April 1954 it flew from St Athan to RAF Hemswell, used as camera aircraft – for the head-on views of the Lancasters in *The Dambusters* film. Returned to St Athan in October and SOC, it was grounded and deemed 'non-effective aircraft'. On 24 January 1955 it made the last ever flight of a Wellington, being sold to Vickers Ltd and flown from St Athan to Wisley. Several years in storage followed in various conditions at different locations, before arriving at RAFC in 1971. In 1981 a front gun turret was refitted.

Bristol Aeroplane Company built the Type 156 Beaufighter heavy multi-role aircraft for RAF. This 1944 Mark X was built at Old Mixon, near Weston-super-Mare (allocated serial number RD 253). TOC with RAF, between 13 and 22 March 1945 it was one of sixteen ferried to Portela, Lisbon, for use by Portuguese Naval Air Arm on maritime patrol duties. SOC in 1949, it was used at Lisbon Technical Institute as an instructional airframe until 1965. Presented to RAF for preservation, it arrived at Bicester by July that year. Restoration began in 1967, completed by 1968, and in 1971 it transferred to RAFH. It is pictured on 5 January 2024.

De Havilland Aircraft Co. DH.98 Mosquito twin-engined multi-role combat aircraft were primarily used by the RAF. Built in July 1945, this B35 type (serial No. TJ 138), TOC with RN, by the end of August that year had transferred to RAF Shawbury for storage. In February 1948 it moved to Martlesham Heath in Suffolk – for reasons unknown to the author. In May 1948 it returned to RAF Shawbury and went into storage again. In October 1950 it transferred to Fassberg, West Germany. In February 1951 it was back in the UK at RAF Llandow, again in storage. In 1953 it was sent to Brooklands Aviation at Sywell and converted to a TT.35, followed by a period of six years serving at various RAF installations until declared non-effective aircraft in July 1959 and SOC. Under ownership of AHB in May 1960 until donated to the RAFH in 1992, it is seen on 5 January 2024.

The Messerschmitt ME262 German fighter/fighter-bomber. This March 1945 example, a 262A-2a Sturmvogel fighter-bomber variant, TOC with Luftwaffe, serial number I./JG7, was captured by Allies at Fassberg in June 1945 and transported the 1,118 miles by road/sea to Brize Norton (via Copenhagen) for evaluation purposes. RAF hierarchy were impressed and it was TOC on test flights for pilot training purposes, serial number VK 893. Its final flight occurred on 29 November 1945, some eight months after leaving the factory. SOC in 1946, it was displayed at various RAF bases throughout the UK and on display in 1976 at RAFH. Moved between RAFH and RAFC on about a half a dozen or so occasions, it was noted at RAFC on 23 December 2023.

B-25 Mitchell twin-engined medium bombers were capable of carrying 2,400-lb payloads. Developed by North American Aviation for USAAF, this example (serial number 44-31171) was built in 1945, TOC, and SOC in October 1958. Following a brief period in open storage, it was in service with Radio Corporation of America, civilian registration N7614C, for detecting damage to radio masts and radar stations at remote locations. Between 1970 and 1976 it was used by Euramericair Incorporated and fitted with a modified camera nose for taking aerial photographs. Withdrawn from use in 1974, it ended up in open storage at Shoreham Airport for two years, then acquired by IWMD in 1976. On 23 September 2023 it was suspended from the ceiling in American Air Museum.

Chapter Four

The Cold War, 1946–91

The Cold War came about when two of the world's superpowers, America and Russia, had an uneasy alliance in which tensions increased, with both nations supporting opposing sides (supplying weapons and equipment, training of troops, etc.) in 'proxy wars'.

The term 'Cold War' comes from the fact that both America and Russia would not become involved in major conflicts with each other. The chapter features aircraft built during those forty-five years. There were many different conflicts that took place during this period, such as the Malayan Emergency, Mau Mau Uprising, Korean War, Vietnam War, Suez Crisis, Tibetan Uprising (both Americans and Russians supported the same sides in the last two conflicts above), Aden Emergency, Congo Crisis, Communist Insurgencies of Thailand and Malaya, Cambodian-Vietnamese War, Soviet-Afghan War, Falklands War and First Iraq War, with many other conflicts also taking place. The Cold War officially ended with the dissolution of the former Soviet Union in 1991.

The RAF had a lack of sufficient aircraft to be deployed in the Pacific, so A.V. Roe designed and manufactured an enlarged version of the Lancaster – the Type 64 Lincoln four-engined heavy bomber, first flown three days after the D-Day landings. This B2 version, finished in 1945, just a little too late to see service in the Second World War, TOC with RAF, serial number RF 398, served for twelve years, seeing action in 1950 against Malayan terrorists and against the Mau-Mau in Kenya in 1953. In 1960 it was involved in radar development trials until SOC in 1963, when it made the last ever flight of a Lincoln bomber to RAF Henlow. In 1973 it was on display at RAFC and is pictured on 23 December 2023.

The 510 (Swift) prototype interceptor jet fighter was built by Supermarine Aviation. The type itself suffered from a protracted technical issue during development. VV 106 (built in 1948), TOC with RAEB, in March 1949 made a wheels-up crash landing after the undercarriage gear failed to operate. In 1950 it was modified by RAEF for naval use and was involved in deck trials on board HMS *Illustrious*. On 9 November that year, it swung on take-off, the wing tips damaging a gun turret. In November 1952 at Farnborough it made another wheels-up crash landing, the undercarriage failing to operate again. In January 1955 all of the type were SOC and withdrawn (due to repeated mechanical failures). A period of forty years in storage at various RAF locations followed. Donated to FAAM in 1995, it is seen in the reserve collection at Cobham Hall on 5 September 2019.

Skyraider AD-4W attack aircraft were manufactured by Douglas Aircraft Co. This example, a three-seater, was fitted with the AN/APS-20 airborne early warning anti-submarine, maritime surveillance and weather radar system. Built in 1951, it was TOC with USN and its serial number was 124121. In September 1953, it was TOC with RN and its serial number was WT 983 (carrying WT 121, applied in error), then redesignated an AEW.1. In 1974 it attended the air show at Old Warden. SOC in 1979, in 1980 it was displayed at the newly opened Swiss Air Force Museum in Dubendorf, remaining for twelve years. Donated to FAAM in 1992 and bought to the UK, it is pictured at Cobham Hall on 5 September 2019.

De Havilland Aircraft Co. of Canada produced the DHC-1 Chipmunk tandem single-engined training aircraft. This example (T.20 type), pictured at the C&LR on 24 April 2011, was built in Portugal during 1952 and TOC with Portuguese Air Force, serving until 1955, transferring to the Department of Defence at Gormanston Military Camp, Ireland, with serial number 173. In 1974 it transferred to Irish Air Corps at Casement Aerodrome until the early 1990s. SOC and privately purchased, it was taken to New Ross prior to moving to Dromod.

The 1-131E Jungmann was built under licence by Construcciones Aeronauticas S.A. (CASA) in Spain. This example, a training aircraft, was built in 1954 for Spanish Air Force, serial number E.3B-209, serving until late 1980s despite being an outdated biplane. In 1988 it was in storage on the outskirts of Madrid in a hangar, then purchased by a collector in January 1990, civilian registration G-BSAJ. In April 1991 it was issued with a certificate of airworthiness, enabling it to take part in air shows. Seen on 23 September 2023 at IWMD.

Serial number WJ 639, built by Handley Page in 1954, was an English Electric Canberra B.2 medium bomber. TOC with RAF, it was converted to a TT.18. In January 1971 it was at British Aircraft Corporation (BAC) Warton for trial installation to assess its banner-towing capability. In July that year it transferred to A&AEE – until September, when it transferred to BAC Samlesbury for modifications. SOC in January 1973, it was sold to Flight Refuelling Ltd in Wimborne. In the late 1970s it was retaken back on charge with RAF, serving until December 1981, then transferred to BAe at Farnborough. In June 1988 it was purchased by NELSAM, transported there by road. Pictured on 19 October 2014.

Blackburn Beverley B-101 heavy transport aircraft could carry up to ninety-two fully equipped paratroopers. Serial number XB 259 (sole survivor out of forty-nine), built in 1955 and TOC with RAF, served until 1967 (SOC). Acquired privately in 1968 and given civilian registration G-AOAI, its last flight was in 1974. In 1983 it was donated to the Museum of Army Transport at Beverley, remaining for twenty years. In 2003 it was purchased and transported by road to Napoleonic Fort Paull Museum in Hull (seen on 6 October 2018). When the museum closed in 2020 it was partly dismantled and moved to RAF Riccall. In January 2024, Solway Aviation Museum purchased it for eventual display at the Carlisle Lake District Airport.

Sited within metres of the main runway at Gatwick Airport is GAMC. Prominent in the 'open space' at the rear is a 1958 Avro Shackleton MR.3 maritime patrol craft, serial number WR 982, TOC with RAF. In 1964 it underwent major modifications at Boscombe Down – including bomb-bay heating, auxiliary fuel tank jettisoning and special stores drop facilities.

In 1965 it was ferried to the Moray Firth, then subsequently to RAF Kinloss. In 1967 it was fitted with an STR 70 radar altimeter weather detector. SOC in 1970, it was transferred to RAF Cosford as an instructional airframe until 1988. It was acquired by GAMC when the MoD put it up for sale.

Gloster Aircraft Co. Javelin all-weather fighter-interceptors. This 1958 example, built as FAW.7 and TOC with RAF, carried serial number XH 897. In 1960 it was converted for chase and calibration duties to FAW.9. The work was completed in 1961 and it was allocated to RAF Benson. In 1967 it was transferred to A&AEE for calibrating the supersonic measurements of the upcoming Concorde project. It was the last Javelin to fly, its final flight occurring on 24 January 1975 when it flew to IWMD before SOC. Seen on 23 September 2023.

French manufacturer Dassault Aviation SA built the MD.454 Mystere IV fighter-bomber for the French Air Force. Serial number 146, built in 1956, TOC, served with five different squadrons and carried six different serial numbers. SOC in 1977, in 1978 it was stored by Experimental Aircraft Association (EAA.601) at RAF Sculthorpe, having flown a total of 4,255 hours since being built. In 1981 it was donated to NELSAM, arriving in May 1982. Pictured on 19 October 2014.

One of the most iconic-looking planes to come out of the 1960s: the Avro-built Vulcan B.2 strategic bomber. It had fourteen fuel tanks with a capacity to carry 11,250 gallons, a range of 2,601 miles, and could carry a payload of 21,000 lbs of explosives.

XH 558, built in 1960, was TOC with RAF at Finningley until 1968 with a squadron that specialised in training Vulcan pilots. In 1973 it was converted to a B.2 (MRR) but was laid up damaged from November 1975 until October 1976. Back into service and further converted to a K.2 in 1982, it operated in this guise until 1985, then reconverted back to a standard B.2. In 1983 it was part of 'Vulcan Display Team', until SOC and subsequently grounded in 2015. Its last flight occurred on 28 October that year, seen flying over Kemble airfield, bomb doors open, on an impromptu unscheduled fly past during the Gloucestershire Steam Extravaganza being held on 7 August 2010.

Designed during the latter years of the Second World War, the Lockheed P-2 Neptune maritime patrol and anti-submarine warfare craft entered service in 1947. Number 204, built in 1961 as P2V-7B – special variant for Royal Netherlands Navy – served with them for twenty-one years. SOC in 1982, the last operational Dutch Neptune made its last flight to RAFC in July of that year. Noted on 23 December 2023.

The 35 Draaken supersonic single-seater fighter-interceptor jet aircraft was built by Svenska Aeroplan Aktiebolaget (SAAB) for use with Swedish, Austrian, Finnish and Royal Danish Air Forces. They had two unusual features: the double delta-shaped wing, which reduced take-off run, and double wheels at the rear of the fuselage in order to stop the extra-long tail scraping the runway. They had a top speed of Mach 2.3 (1,534 mph) and a range of 1,710 miles. This 1961-built Model A, TOC with Swedish Air Force and serial number Fv35075, was assigned to Flygflottily (Fighter Wing) F16 at Uppsala, serving until SOC in 1977. Donated to IWMD, staying there until 2005, it transferred to D&GM, outside of Dumfries, and is seen on 23 October 2024.

The SR-71 Blackbird, developed in the late 1950s/early 1960s by Lockheed Corporation for USAF, was a long-range, high-altitude Mach3+ (2,200 mph) strategic reconnaissance craft. Thirty-two were built and they had a range of 3,250 miles. Featuring some of the earliest forms of stealth technology – sharp edges and smooth lines between the fuselage and wings and black paint to make it virtually undetectable. This one, TOC with USAF in 1962, serial number 61-7962, served until SOC in 1999. It then became property of National Museum of USAF based at Wright Field in Daytona. In April 2001 it was loaned to IWMD and put on display in American Air Museum. Seen on 23 September 2023.

In 1963 this Buccaneer S.1 Maritime Strike aircraft left the Blackburn Aircraft factory, serial number XN 957 and TOC with RN. Between then and 1974 it served with three RN squadrons, spending its entire military career based at Lossiemouth. After serving with the RN for eleven years and racking up 900 flying hours it was SOC in 1974 and acquired by FAAM. Pictured in the 'Aircraft Carrier' Hall on 16 December 2023.

PZL Swidnik was the largest aircraft manufacturer in Poland, and during the interwar period it became PZL Warszawa. Built in 1964 under licence was serial number 1420, a Lim-2 fighter jet based on the Russian MiG-15.TOC with Polish Air Force and SOC in 1986. It was acquired by film company Aces High Ltd and given the civilian registration G-BMZF. In May 1987 it was donated to FAAM and its civilian registration was cancelled in 1990. Seen on 16 December 2023, sporting North Korean colours representing those flown during the Korean War.

The Gnat fighter, light tactical bomber and training aircraft was built by Folland Aircraft and served with RAF for over twenty years, mostly for training purposes. The T.1 variant gained prominence as the craft used by the Red Arrows Display Team for several years. This 1962 T.1 example, TOC with RAF and serial number XP 504, in 1978 was given the new serial number 8618M, remaining as an instructional airframe until SOC in 1991. Privately purchased, it was given the civilian registration G-TIMM. Ownership passed to Swept Wing Ltd of Milton Keynes in 2008, who repainted it (with permission from RAF) into the Red Arrows colours of the 1960s/70s, with serial number XS 111. In hindsight it was not the best idea, as the original XS 111 was destroyed in a 1976 crash at Kemble Airport – no casualties. This incarnation fared much worse, crashing during a display at CarFest North, Oulton Park, on 1 August 2015 – the craft was destroyed and sadly the pilot died. Seen on display at the RIAT on 18 July 2010.

A staple aircraft of the Cold War was English Electric interceptor-fighter jet the Lightning – with their unique vertical staggered configuration of twin engines within the fuselage. This example, an F.6, was built in 1966 and TOC with RAF, serial number XR 771 to RAF Leuchars. It also served at RAF Luqa in Malta, used on test and evaluation trials, and at RAF Binbrook. SOC in 1988, its final flight occurred on 23 March that year, flying from Binbrook to Baginton Airfield. Displayed at the MAM, it is pictured on Christmas Eve 2023.

Hawker-Siddeley ground attack and recconnaissance fighter jet the Harrier GR (nicknamed 'Jump- Jet') was the first and most successful aircraft fitted with vertical take-off and landing (VTOL) equipment. This example (serial number XV 741) was built in 1968 as GR.3, TOC with RAF. In May 1969 it won the Daily Mail Transatlantic Air Race on the 50th Anniversary of the first transatlantic air crossing, completed in 6 hours 11 minutes.

In 1991 it was a training/instructional airframe with HMS Seahawk at RNAS Culdrose until 2008, when it transferred to HMS Sultan at Gosport, still an instructional airframe. SOC in 2011, it was purchased privately, restored, and in April 2019 donated to the BAMM. Seen on 28 May 2022.

Anglo-French manufacturer SEPECAT built the supersonic jet attack aircraft Jaguar. This 1975 example, serial number XX 763, was built by BAC and initially retained by them for publicity duties. TOC with RAF at RAF Lossiemouth, in 1993 it went into storage at RAF Shawbury. In 1995 it moved to RAF St Athan for ground training and was given serial number 9009M. SOC in 2005, it was stored in 2007, then purchased by Transworld Aviation Trading. After a couple more years in storage, it arrived at the BAM in 2009. Pictured on 2 April 2022.

British Aircraft Corporation 167 Strikemaster light attack and training aircraft were initially built exclusively for Royal Saudi Air Force (RSAF), but were also used by Ecuadorian, Kenyan and New Zealand air forces. Serial number 1133, built in January 1977, a '80A' variant, and TOC with RSAF in July that year, serving with them until SOC in 2001. In 2002 it was donated to IWMD. Pictured on 23 September 2023.

In order to quell rebel operations in 1966, the Argentinian government instructed Fabrica Militar de Aviones to manufacture a ground attack and counter-insurgency craft. The result was the IA 58 Pucara, which had a cockpit floor layered with armoured material and a bulletproof windscreen. Built exclusively for Argentinian Air Force (AAF), this example, serial number A-522, built in 1980, served with AAF at the outbreak of the Falklands War in 1982. When the war ended eleven were captured by allied forces, six of which were transported to the UK. This one was moved by road from Southampton to RAF Abingdon, and some of the parts were removed in order to complete one in flying condition by A+AEE. In December it was sent to FAAM, displayed until 1994, loaned to NELSAM, and is pictured on 19 October 2014.

Panavia Tornado twin-engined variable swept wing multi-role combat aircraft, a joint development between Britain, Germany and Italy, were built at Panavia Aircraft Ltd, Germany. Serial number ZA 765, built in 1983 as GR.1 and TOC with RAF at St Athan, moved to RAF Laarbruch, Germany, until 1987. Transferred to RAF Marham for a few months between May and October 1987, it served with six different squadrons based at Laarbruch and RAF Bruggen in Germany. Serving during the 1991 Gulf War (operating from Saudi Arabia), it carried out two runway denials, twenty-eight free falls and fourteen laser-guided bombing missions. Following that war it was redeployed to the famous 'Dambusters' Squadron, modified in 1997 to GR.1B, fitted with the Sea-Eagle anti-ship missile, and based at RAF Lossiemouth. SOC in 2001, it transferred to IWMD in 2002 and is pictured on 23 September 2023.

Chapter Five

Second Cold War, 1992–Present Day

The period that followed the Cold War included the major conflicts in the ongoing Angolan Civil War, Yugoslav Wars and the increased rise of threats from growing terrorists movements – such as Al-Qaeda, ISIS, Hamas and the Taliban – which all came to a shocking head on 9 September 2001 with the attacks on the World Trade Centre and Pentagon in America (commonly referred to as the 9/11 attacks). This resulted in many ongoing air strikes regularly taking place in mostly Middle Eastern countries who were either harbouring or supporting those terrorist factions.

The twenty-first century has continued to see air forces from most of the western and eastern parts of the world manufacture the latest high-technology aircraft, so that they are ready to face any hostilities from any faction if required to do so. Especially considering that there are numerous ongoing conflicts which continue to cause unrest in many parts of the world, such as the ongoing Israeli/Hamas war in the Gaza strip and the war between Russia and the Ukraine.

In 1989 Short Brothers were instructed to come up with a two-seater basic training aircraft; the result was the turboprop jet Tucano T.1. This example, ZF 317, built in 1992 and TOC with RAF at RAF Marham, was with a once historically famous bomber squadron (later communications and training squadron), remaining until SOC in 2019. Sold to a private buyer, as of July 2022 it has been in private storage somewhere in the Kent area. Seen here on 18 July 2010 taking part in the RIAT.

McConnell-Douglas built the F/A-18F Super Hornet supersonic twin-engined carrier multi-role fighter aircraft for USN. They had the capability to carry thirty-four various air-to-air or thirty-three various air-to-surface missiles or a combination of both. This 1995 example, TOC with USN, serial number 166923, flew with various strike fighter squadrons based at Lenmoore air base in California and in Iwakuni, Japan. Seen preparing to take off on 18 July 2010 at the RIAT.

Multinational-built Eurofighter EF2000 Typhoon delta wing supersonic multirole air superiority jet fighters. This example is ZH 588, built in 1993 and TOC with MoD at BAE Warton. Undergoing various engine tests, its first flight didn't happen until April the following year. In 1995 it was still used by BAE at Warton for test flying. Its last flight occurred in January 2007 at RAF Coningsby, after which it was used as a spare parts source. In November that year it was dismantled and delivered by road to RAF Brize Norton, then in December was being used for air portability trials for the upcoming USAF Boeing C-17 Globemaster III Transport aircraft. In January 2008, it was transferred by road to the RAFH, and by 2009 it was suspended from the ceiling. Pictured on 5 January 2024.

Built jointly by Bell Helicopter & Boeing Defense, the tiltrotor military transport aircraft V-22 Osprey has VTOL capabilities, designed to combine the vertical take-off ability of a helicopter with the range of a fixed wing craft. It has twin rotors (one on the end of each wing), which rotate from a horizontal to a vertical position and vice-versa. Serial number 11-0058, built in 2008 and TOC with 7th Special Operations Squadron, was based at RAF Mildenhall. Seen on 2 April 2022 with its rotors in mid-tilt, making an impromptu unscheduled flypast over BAM.

With a total of eight test craft and 187 production models built by Lockheed Martin Aeronautics in Fort Worth, the F-22 Raptor stealth superiority fighter aircraft was primarily used with USAF. Serial number 06-4126 was built in 2006 and TOC with USAF, but little is known of its military history to the author. Pictured on 18 July 2010 taking part in the RIAT, shortly after take-off in a demonstration display.

Weighing over 77 tons, the Airbus A400M Atlas strategic and tactical transport aircraft was used by RAF, French, German and Spanish air forces. This 2008 example was the second prototype, with serial number EC-402, which made its first public appearance at the 2010 RIAT (seen on 18 October during a demonstration flight). These huge beasts can carry a payload weighing up to 37 tons. The project was nearly cancelled due to programme development delays and cost overruns. However, the customer nations stuck with it and by 2011, 174 had been ordered for eight different nations – it is worth noting, however, that by 31 July 2024 only 127 had actually been built.

Chapter Six

Seaplanes

In 1876 Frenchman Alphonse Penaud filed the first patent for an aircraft with a boat hull and retractable landing gear. However, Austrian Wilhelm Kress is credited with actually building the first seaplane in 1898, although its two 30-hp Daimler engines were inadequate for take-off and it sank when one of its two floats collapsed.

The word seaplane is used to describe two types of air/water craft: 1. Floatplane – which has slender floats (usually two) beneath the fuselage; 2. A flying-boat – where the main source of buoyancy is the fuselage itself, which is shaped and acts like a ship's hull in the water, due to its hydrodynamical shape.

Above left: The Sopwith Baby single-seater scouting and bomber float biplane was built by Sopwith Aviation Co. and used by RNAS. This example at FAAM on 16 December 2023 is a composite constructed of the fuselage and engine from serial number 8214 and wings, floats other parts from 8215, both built in 1916 and sent to Italy to be used as patterns for licence-built craft. The parts were found in a BEA hangar at London airport in 1960. In 1966 they were combined as this single craft prior to going to FAAM in 1970.

Above right: This Supermarine Southampton MkI was one of six wooden-hulled submarines built in 1925. TOC with RAF at Gosport, it was used on various missions until November 1926. On 23 November 1928 a storm forced three Southamptons to break free of their moorings at Portland (this one and two metal-hulled versions); this one smashed into breakwater, wrecking the wings and part of the hull – the other two sank.

The remains of the hull were purchased in 1929, repaired and converted to a houseboat on the tidal mud flats of the River Deben. In 1966 the local council ordered it disposed of, so it was sold to RAFM for £75 in 1967. It went to the museum workshop's store until 1984, when restoration began, which was completed in 1995. It is on display at RAFH and pictured on 5 January 2024.

Spitfire designer Reginald Joseph Mitchell also designed the single-engine amphibious biplane Supermarine Walrus, primarily used on maritime patrol duties. They served extensively with RN, RAF, Irish Air Corps and RAAF. This 1939 example (serial number L2301) for FAA was diverted and TOC with Irish Air Corps. In January 1942, four Irish Nationals stole it and attempted to join the Luftwaffe, but were intercepted by Spitfires and escorted to St Eval in Cornwall. Following the war and SOC, it was sold to Irish Airline Company Aer Lingus and re-registered EI-ACC, but never entered service with them. TOC in 1947 with Royal Auxiliary Air Force, it was used at bathing parties. SOC in 1948, a year later it was noted on a dump in Thame. In 1963 it was purchased for £5 and donated to FAAM. Sent to Royal Naval Engineering College at Arbroath in 1964 for restoration, which was completed in 1966, it returned to Yeovilton. Seen on 16 December 2023.

Serial number 63993 was built by Consolidated Vultee in April 1945. TOC with USN, it served with different branches of Fleet Air Wing until 1957. Transferred to Denmark for Royal Danish Air Force (RDAF), serial number 82-866, it was used for parachuting provisions and mail to isolated radio and weather stations. It suffered minor damage in 1958 when the nose wheel collapsed. In 1962 and 1963 it was involved in birdstrikes, causing more damage, and in 1968 it struck an iceberg whilst on a sortie, receiving major damage to the nose section. Grounded at an isolated outpost, it was temporarily repaired and flew to Mestersuig where a full repair took place. In November 1970 it was the last PBY-6A Catalina to be SOC from RDAF. On 30 May 1974 it made its last ever flight, journeying from Vaerlose to RAF Colerne. Arriving at RAFC in 1976, it is seen on 23 December 2023.

Short S.25 Sunderland flying boat patrol bombers were developed and constructed exclusively for RAF. This example, serial number ML 824, was built in 1944, a Sunderland III, and TOC with RAF, at Wig Bay, Stranraer, and later that year was converted to a GR.5. During 1945 it served in Northern Ireland and Sullom Voe, Shetland Islands. It flew its last operational flight of the Second World War on 13 May 1945. It was then stored at RAF Alness until 1948, then prepared for the Berlin Airlift but not used. In August 1950, TOC with French Air Force, it served with them in Dakar and Senegal, West Africa, until 1956. Transferred to the French Navy, its last flight with them was in 1960. In 1971 it was moved by road and barge to Pembroke Dock, dismantled, and delivered to RAFH, arriving in March. The end of month saw the beginning of the airframe being reconstructed, which was completed in September 1976. On display in 1983, it is seen on 5 January 2024.

The maritime reconnaissance flying boat Supermarine Stranraer was the last and fastest biplane flying boat used by the RAF. This version was built under licence by Canadian Vickers in 1940, TOC with RCAF and serial number 920. Serving with four different squadrons, it was SOC in May 1944. From 1944 to 1947 its owners were Labrador Mining & Exploration Co. and had the civilian registered CF-BXO. It was loaned to Canadian Pacific Airlines during 1944. In 1947 it was owned by Canadian Queen Charlotte Airlines. In 1949 it struck a submerged tree trunk during take-off. The damage was repaired in 1950 and it was converted to a 'Super' Stranraer. Withdrawn in 1952, it was in open storage at Vancouver until 1958, then acquired by Stranraer Aerial Enterprises Ltd. In 1962 on Seers Lake it hit a rock, damaging the hull, sinking in the shallow water. Temporarily repaired, it was flown to Vancouver for extensive repairs. Between 1963 and 1966 it was leased to Pacific Western Airlines, then withdrawn and in open storage in Vancouver until 1968. RAFM purchased it in 1970, arriving at RAFH in 1971. Pictured on 5 January 2024.

Chapter Seven

Gliders

Gliders have been used by air forces in various countries since the 1940s for use in transporting infantry and heavy equipment into combat zones. One of the main use of gliders within air forces throughout the world has also been for pilot training and by air cadets.

The GAL.49 Hamilcar Mark 1 British Military heavy cargo glider was built by General Aircraft. There are no complete survivors. This example, serial number TK 777, was built in 1944 and TOC with the British Army, taking part in operations in the Netherlands and Germany. Serving with Glider Pilot Regiment until 1956 and SOC, its forward fuselage and cockpit were sold off and used as a lambing shed and chicken coop respectively. Its fuselage was rescued by MAF – the cockpit was deemed too far gone – during the late 1990s, and with its replica partial wings, it is the most complete example of this type. Pictured on 17 August 2024.

Seen at MAF on 17 August 2024, this is a complete example of a WACO CG-4 Hadrian American military troop/cargo carrying glider. Built under licence by Gliders & Airplanes in 1942, CG-4A, TOC with USAAF, serial number 42-43809, could carry twelve troops. It was one of 136 taking part in an operation in Sicily; tragedy occurred when sixty-five were released early by their towing craft, with the loss of 252 lives. Uncertain when SOC, it was donated to the museum in 1985, from collection in France. Loading of this craft was done via the upward-lifting hinged cockpit section.

These training gliders were mainly constructed of wood, large proportions of which were made by furniture makers in department stores. Airspeed Ltd were responsible for manufacturing Horsa gliders. This example, an AS.51, serial number KJ 351, was built in 1945, TOC with AAC, and had capacity to carry thirty troops. Coming in at 88 feet long makes it one of the longest troop gliders built. It served with AAC Glider Pilot Regiment until the mid-1950s, then transferred to RCAF to participate in evaluation trials. SOC in 1968, it was acquired by Assault Glider Trust at MAF. Noted on 17 August 2024.

Several Horsa and Hamilcar fuselages were sold on after the war to farmers, etc., for chicken coops, animal shelters and even housing. This Horsa MkII saw further use on a farm in Wiltshire, both the fuselage and cockpit being used on the same farm. The two parts were purchased in 2004 by MAF and reassembled, showing the folding cockpit and loading ramps from another Horsa MkII, making a very good representation of how it would have looked when loading/unloading. Pictured on 17 August 2024.

General Aircraft produced Hotspur gliders. Manufacturing had begun when they were deemed unsuitable for operational use, as they were only able to carry eight troops. They became the main training glider of the Second World War. This composite example is comprised of the main fuselage from 1942-built serial number HH 279, and parts from other craft. It is the only complete surviving example. The parts began to be assembled by MAF in 1995, making its display debut in 2001. Seen on 17 August 2024.

Slingsby Aviation was founded in 1930 by a former First World War RAF pilot solely for the purpose of designing and building gliders and sailplanes. Producing over fifty different types, many saw service with RAF and AAC. One of the oldest known surviving Slingsby gliders can be seen on display at MAF (pictured on 17 August 2024). This Kirby Kite T.6 was built in 1936, TOC with RAF, serial number G 285. After the hostilities of the Second World War ended and it was SOC, it was purchased by Ulster Gliding Club and given the civilian registration G-ALNH. It was acquired from them in 1989 by MAF. Only twenty-five of these were built.

Kirby T.8 Tutor gliders were sixty-two conversions of the Kirby T.7 Cadet. This example, serial number VW 529, was built in 1947 and TOC with ATC. It was later renumbered to XE 759. SOC in 1957, it was sold to an unknown gliding club, then acquired by SYAM during 2017. Pictured on 30 August 2021.

The Slingsby T.30 Prefect intermediate training glider was used by the RAF. Fifty-three were built. This 1950 example, serial number WE 987 and TOC with the RAF and ATC, served with three different squadrons. In 1972 it transferred to Newport Pagnall Air Cadets Corps Gliding School, serial number BGA.2517. SOC in 1989 and placed into storage, it was acquired in 2001 by SYAM. Seen on 30 August 2021.

RAF primary training glider T.38 Grasshopper.115s were built by Slingsby. The design of these was based on a pre-Second World War German model with modified Kirby T.7 Cadet wings. Serial number WZ 791 was built in 1952, TOC with RAF and SOC in 1991. Donated to RAFH, it is pictured on 5 November 2016.

The Kirby T.31B Tandem Tutor was a two-seater development of the Kirby Tutor T.8, with 230 constructed. XA 282, built in 1952 and TOC with ATC, served with three different squadrons. SOC in 1986, it was purchased by CAAM. It is pictured on 20 April 2019, clearly showing the tandem seating configuration.

Chapter Eight

Helicopters

The first recorded manned flight of a helicopter took place in August/September 1907, when 'Gyroplane No.1', built by the French brothers Jacques and Louis Breguet, lifted its pilot approximately 2 feet into the air and held him there for one minute. However, the first recorded 'truly manned free flight' went to the honour of fellow French inventor Paul Cornu in November of that year, when his craft – the 'Cornu' helicopter – lifted its pilot 1 foot in the air and held him there for twenty seconds. But in all reality the distinction of first manned helicopter flight must be accredited to the Breguet brothers. Helicopters have progressed dramatically in their design, purpose and ability during the last 117 years.

Sikorsky R-4 Hoverfly was the first helicopter to serve with USAAF and RAF. 133 were built. This 1944 example was built by Sikorsky Aircraft as R-4B, TOC with USAAF and serial number 43-46596, and flown to Newark. In January 1945, TOC with RAF and serial number KL 110, it was sent to Hooton Park. In March that year it transferred to RAF Hawarden and into storage until October, then flew to RAF Andover. In 1947 it transferred to the Kings Flight – deployed as a mail carrier to and from RAF Dyce and Balmoral Castle. TOC with RN in 1949 and SOC in 1966, it was offered to RAFH, arriving in 1970. Pictured on 5 January 2024.

In 1947 Westland Aircraft began manufacturing, under licence, an Anglicised version of the Sikorsky H-5; the result was the WS-51 Dragonfly. 149 were built for training, air-sea rescue and communications roles, and were the first helicopters produced by Westland. This example was built in 1952, a HR.3, and TOC with RN FAA in Gosport.

Converted to a HR.5 in 1957, it continued serving with FAA until 1967. In store until 1970 and SOC, it was sold to Twyford Moors Ltd. Purchased privately in 1973, it was loaned to FAAM until 1976, then sent to Weston-super-Mare for partial refurbishment. Loaned to RAF Central Flying School and further restored, it was returned to its original silver livery and on display at HCM in 1989. Seen on 28 September 2023.

In 1955 Westland improved the WS-51, modifying three of them, which became the Widgeon Series 2. Never intended to be a military craft, an order for another twelve was completed for the Brazilian Navy and Biafran Air Force – it is with the latter this example has a connection. In 1957 it was civilian-registered G-AOZE, then sold to Bristow Helicopters. In 1960 it was shipped to Bahrain to ferry personnel to/from offshore oil rigs in the Persian Gulf. In 1962 it was transferred to Port Harcourt in Nigeria, re-registered 5N-ABW, and allocated to Shell/BP for oil support work. In August 1967 during the Nigerian Civil War, it was captured by Biafran Air Force and flown about a dozen times. It was recovered by the Nigerian army in early September – making it one of the shortest periods served in a military capacity for an aircraft. In 1970 it was returned to Bristows at Redhill and donated to Warden Park School in Cuckfield, then rebuilt, restored and sold to HCM in 1986. Pictured on 28 September 2023.

Piasecki Helicopter Corporation's twin overlapping tandem rotor utility HUP Retriever was introduced in 1949. This 1951 HUP-3 was TOC with USAF, serial number 51-16622, and by 1967 it was TOC with Royal Canadian Navy (RCN), serial number 622. SOC by the mid-1970s, it was purchased privately and given civilian registration N6699D. In 1991 it changed ownership and was on display at HCM – in its RCN livery. Despite changing owners twice since then, it still remains on display, seen on 28 September 2023.

The Westland WS-55 Whirlwind was another Anglicised, built under licence Sikorsky craft, H-19 Chickasaw, used by RN and RAF for anti-submarine and search and rescue roles. This 1954 HAR.1 left Westlands, TOC with RN, serial number XA 870, and was an Antarctic patrol vehicle. Transferred in 1966 to Air Engineering School, serial number A2543 RAF, it served until SOC in 1973. Later that year it was displayed at SYAM. Pictured on 30 August 2021.

The Type 171 Sycamore was built by Bristol Aeroplane Co. for both military and civilian use. Serial number XL 829 was the last one TOC with RAF and the last one to be withdrawn from service. Built in 1957 as a rescue and anti-submarine craft, it was in a support role for the SAS at El Adem, Libya, in 1958. It served with Search & Rescue Flight in Aden until 1964, returning to the UK on board HMS *Albion*. Transferred to RAF Metropolitan Communications Squadron, it was used on VIP duties. SOC in 1971, it was acquired by City of Bristol Museum, flown from RAF Northolt to Bristol Lulsgate Airport, and transported to the museum by road. In storage until 1978, it was on display at the Industrial Museum until 2006. Donated to HCM, arriving in 2008, it is seen on 28 September 2023.

The light utility Mi-1 Type 32 HARE was produced by Mil Helicopters. This 1959, built under licence by PZL Swidnik example, TOC with Polish Air Force and serial number 2007, was used for pilot training until the late 1980s, when SOC. Acquired by HCM in 1993, it is pictured on 28 September 2023 carrying Soviet Union colours.

Introduced in 1953, the Mil Mi-4 Type 36 HOUND transport helicopter was Russia's answer to the Wessex Whirlwind. This 1957 example, TOC with Czech Air Force and serial number 9147, was in an assault transport role, serving until SOC in 1990. In 1992 it became the first Russian helicopter to be preserved in the UK. Purchased by HCM, it is pictured on 28 September 2023.

The Westland Wessex HAS.1 was an Anglicised, built under licence version of the Sikorsky H-34. This example, serial number XS 887, was built in 1966, TOC with RN and allocated to HMS *Fife*. In 1973 it was transferred to RNAS Yeovilton, then allocated to RNAS Portland in 1975. In 1980 it transferred to HMS Seahawk, RNAS Culdrose. SOC in 1982, the following July it was on display at Flambards Holiday Village, Helston. In December 2007 it was moved and displayed at SYAM. Noted on 30 August 2021.

The Westland Wessex HAS.3 was the anti-submarine version of the HAS.1, comprising of three new builds and forty-three converted from HAS.1s, which are easily recognisable by the radar dome on top of the rear fuselage. This example, seen at BAM on 2 April 2022, is a pre-production model that was built in 1965, with serial number XT 257. Having never seen operational service, it spent its military career with A+AEE, for testing flight control systems and radio evaluation. In 1980 it was TOC with RAF, serial number 8719M, an instructional airframe at RAF Halton. During that period it acquired the yellow colour scheme of RAF HAR.2 search and rescue craft but was never used as such. In 1998 it was sold to a private buyer in West Sussex, making its final journey by road in 2005 to its current home.

In 1969 Westland built two Wessex HCC.4s, both painted into a distinguished red and navy livery. Serial number XV 732 was TOC with RAF Royal Queen's Flight, based at RAF Benson. In 1972 it suffered damage; repaired at Bicester, it was sent to Kemble for respraying, then returned to duties by September 1973. SOC in 1998 having made 1,163 flights, it is worth noting that the craft not only carried members of the royal family, but also government ministers and visiting overseas royalty/dignitaries. It was placed into long-term unserviceable storage at RAF Shawbury, but in March 2002 was moved by road to RAFH. Noted on 5 January 2024.

Type 192 Belvedere tandem rotorcargo helicopters were used by RAF. Pictured on 5 January 2024 at RAFH was HC.1, serial number XG 474. Built in 1962 and TOC with RAF, it was one of six created and sent to RAF Seletar in Singapore. In December that year it was detached to the Sultanate of Brunei until March 1963, supporting anti-rebel forces following the revolt. Transferred to Aden in 1964, it served until 1965, then returned to Singapore. Having spent its entire military career abroad, it was returned to the UK in June 1969 on board HMS *Albion* and SOC. Having been donated to RAFM, upon its arrival in August it was put into storage at RAF Henlow, arriving at RAFH in March 1971.

The SaRo P.531 five-seat utility helicopter was introduced in 1959. This 1960 example by Westland, TOC with RAF, serial number XP 165, was initially allocated to take part in manufacturer's trials. In 1963 it transferred to FAA at Yeovilton as a trial installation airframe. Refurbished at White Waltham Airfield in 1964, it transferred to RAEF. Its last flight occurred on 28 May 1971. SOC in August 1971, it was placed into storage. In 1975 it was on display at the Southend Historic Air Museum, then in May 1983 acquired by HCM. Pictured on 28 September 2023.

Westland Helicopters developed the Scout helicopter, from the SaRo P.531, during the early 1960s for the British Army. This example, serial number XP 190, was built in 1961 and TOC with AAC, seeing service in Northern Ireland at the height of the Troubles during the 1970s, and also saw active service during the Falklands War in 1982. SOC in 1984, it was put into storage at RAF Wroughton, then donated to SYAM in the 1980s. Seen on 30 August 2021.

Whilst developing the Scout for the British Army, Westland were producing a shipboard anti-submarine craft for the RN – the Wasp. Built in 1965 and TOC with RN was XT 431, initially put into storage until October 1966 but then allocated to RNAS Portland as a crew training craft. In 1972 it transferred to the frigate HMS *Scylla*, serving until 1976 and transferred to HMS *Jupiter*. Between March 1980 and September 1981 it was based on HMS *Rothesay* in a training role. In October 1981 it was declared surplus to requirements, SOC and sold to British Rotorcraft Museum (later HCM). In 2003 it passed into the hands of Crawley Technical College as a training airframe, then moved to GAMC in 2008. It was sold in 2013 to the BAM. Seen on 2 April 2022.

The Sikorsky MH-53M medium-lift Combat Search and Rescue helicopter. This 1968 example, a S-65/HH-53C, TOC with USAF, serial number 68-8284, was immediately sent to the Vietnam War. In 1980 it was converted to a MH-53M Pave Low IV – with Interactive Defensive Avionics System and Multi-Mission Advanced Tactical Terminal.

In 1990 it took part in Operation Desert Shield – the build-up of American forces ahead of the Gulf War – and in the war itself. It also took part in operations in Bosnia-Herzegovina in 1992 and 1994, and Operation Desert Thunder during the Second Gulf War in 1998. SOC in 2008, it arrived at RAFC in 2009. Seen on 23 December 2023.

Built by Sud Aviation in July 1968, serial number SA330A was an Alouette IV. By October it had arrived at Westland in Yeovil, then converted and rebuilt into a Puma HC.10, serial number XW 241. In 1973 it was acquired by Aero Flight at RAE Bedford and extensively instrumented for a wide range of research and system demonstration purposes. Fitted with specially modified main rotor blades, it took part in various experiments aimed at gaining a better understanding of main rotor blade aerodynamics, between 1981 and 1988. Early in the 1990s it was transferred to QinetiQ and used as an Electro Magnetic Compatibility vehicle until 2007. Donated to FAST, it is seen on 7 September 2024.

Westland Sea King helicopters were originally built for anti-submarine warfare and fitted with systems and a fully computerised flight control to accommodate this. They provided a wide range of services in both RN and RAF – primarily as Search & Rescue craft. In 1970 this example, XV 677, left Westland a HAS.6, TOC with RN. During its service career it served in the Falklands, Gulf, Bosnian, Iraq and Afghanistan wars. SOC in 1999 and arriving at SYAM in 2006, it is pictured on 30 August 2021.

Russian-built Mil Mi 8PS HIP rugged utility craft, the world's most produced helicopter. More than 12,000 have been built to date. Serial number 618, built in 1972 and TOC with Polish Air Force, was an executive transport craft, bearing the red and white national colours. In 1973 it was modified to a Mi-8P, painted into a sand and green camouflage livery, and transferred to Leznica-Wielka, to be used as an air ambulance, airborne command post and troop transport carrier. SOC in 2006, it was in open storage until, following a personal request to the Polish Minister of Defence with help from the Polish Aviation Museum, it was moved by road in various pieces to HCM, arriving in 2007. Restoration was put on hold due to other priority projects, but it was finally reassembled and put on display in 2011. Seen on 28 September 2023.

The Mil Mi-24D HIND was the most heavily armed gunship/attack helicopter of the Cold War. Being larger than contemporary Western attack helicopters, they came with a troop cabin for casualty evacuation and troop insertion, etc. They also had streamlined under nose radar, missile sighting systems, a retractable undercarriage to reduce drag, and titanium armoured cockpits with ballistic-resistant windows. There was no NATO equivalent for this helicopter. Built in 1970, TOC with Soviet Air Force, serial number 06 Red served in the 1980–89 Soviet-Afghan War and the Iran-Iraq War. Acquired from Latvia in 2004 by BAE Systems, it was upgraded for display at that year's SBAC Farnborough show. SOC in 2005, it was purchased by MAM. Pictured on 24 December 2023.

In 1980 the RAF began using the large tandem rotor Boeing Chinook transport helicopter. These craft have a top speed of 200 mph, can carry up to fifty-five troops or twenty-four stretchers and three attendants and can carry a mixed cargo payload of 24,000 lb. They have a unique distinctive sound, which can be heard when in flight long before they are seen. This example, serial number ZA 714, was built in 1982 and TOC with RAF. Immediately deployed in the Falklands War, it also served in the Gulf and Afghanistan wars. In 2018 it took part in assisting the French forces in the Northern Mali conflict. Seen arriving at the Capel Military show on 2 July 2022, visitors could go in the cockpit and rear loading area of the craft. It is expected that these craft will remain in service with the RAF until the mid-2040s.

Above left: Bell Helicopters' AH-1F Cobra was the world's first purpose-built attack helicopter. Equipped with a 20-mm cannon, they could carry up to fourteen 2.75-inch rockets and eight anti-tank missiles – the forerunner of the Apache. One was assessed in 1967 at Middle Wallop, described by service personnel as 'impressive'. Serial number 70-15990, built in 1970 and TOC with the US Army, was deployed in the ongoing Vietnam conflict, and also served with the US forces in Germany and Korea. SOC in 2002, it was acquired by MAF in 2003. Seen on 17 August 2024.

Above right: The AgustaWestland Apache AH-1, the licence-built version of the Boeing AH-64 Longbow, was the first attack helicopter adopted by the British Army. This example, pictured at MAF on 17 August 2024, was built in 2001 and equipped with the Longbow radar, which can find and track targets, monitor airspace and profile the terrain around it. TOC with AAC, it was deployed to Afghanistan. In January 2007 it was one of two Apaches that carried troops on their stub wings into Jugroom Fort, Helmand Province, to rescue a fatally wounded comrade. In 2011 it took part in NATO military intervention in Libya. The Libyan response to this proved ineffectual, despite Gaddafi having 450 rocket launchers at his disposal – not one single NATO craft was shot down. SOC in 2024, it was placed on display in the museum in May that year.

The AgustaWestland AW101 Merlin anti-submarine warfare, medium lift transport, search and rescue utility helicopter (replacements for Westland 'Lynx') entered service with RN in 1999. ZJ 135 (in the foreground at RNAS Yeovilton on 16 December 2023) was built in 2001 and TOC with FAA. It was in action in the Caribbean on counter-narcotics and hurricane support services, on maritime security patrol duties in the Persian Gulf, and served in Iraq providing support to British and coalition forces in the area. The fleet of Merlins are expected to be in service with RN until 2040 at the earliest.

Chapter Nine

Unmanned Craft

The use of unmanned craft is not a new concept; the Germans used the V-1 'flying bombs' for example, which were lethally accurate during the Second World War. In the intervening years the use of unmanned craft by various air forces across the world has increased, but only covers a relatively small selection of vehicles (in comparison with other modes of aircraft), but even so these vehicles were used for different jobs and variations ranging from simple remote-controlled target drones to sophisticated radar-jamming devices.

The most well-known unmanned craft was the V-1 flying bomb, designed by German Ministry of Aviation in 1939, but originally developed in 1935 as a target drone with explosives. These craft were only operational during 1944/45, with a staggering 1,870-lb warhead and top speed of 400 mph. Almost 30,000 were built, more than 9,500 of which were launched against Britain, over 8,000 of those targeted at London, about 2,400 hitting their designated targets. They were known as the 'buzz-bomb' or 'doodlebug', due to sound they made when flying – beginning as a distant humming, followed by a booming roar and then silence; you were regarded as being fairly safe as long as you could hear it but the silence precipitated impending disaster or death. This example was found intact and unlaunched in Germany following the end of hostilities. Donated to IWM in 1946, it is seen at IWMD on 23 September 2023.

Actor Reginald Denny (King Boris in the 1960s Batman TV series) in 1940 founded The Radioplane Company. They specialised in manufacturing remote radio-controlled drones for the American Army, used for air observation and as targets. The most popular drone they produced was the Shelduck BTT (Basic Training Target), with in excess of 76,000 built. This 1942 example, a MQM-36 model, TOC with RAF, serial number XR 346, remained in service as an observational craft until mid-2008. SOC in April 2009, it was donated to BAM. Pictured on 2 April 2022.

The QH-50 DASH drone anti-submarine helicopter was built by Gyrodyne Co. These lightweight unmanned craft could carry two torpedoes – each with a 75-lb warhead and a top speed of 92 mph. This example, serial number 1482, built in 1966 and TOC with USN, was used in the Vietnam War providing live video feed to ships' captains, directing them where to aim their missiles at on-shore targets. Following that conflict, it was on board a modernised destroyer, which provided improved sonar for tracking submarines. Transferred to the US Army in 1974 and SOC in the 1980s, it was then purchased by a collector. In 2013 it was spotted in a scrapyard in Bakersfield, then purchased by HCM, arriving in 2014. Seen on 28 September 2023.

The MQM-74A Chukar 1 recoverable remote-controlled subsonic aerial target. Built by Northrop Grumann Corporation, over 1,800 were purchased by RN. These target drones had a neatly tapered cigar-shaped fuselage, mid-mounted wings, an underslung jet engine, and were capable of speeds of up to Mach 0.86 (660 mph). Chukar was an Asian species of partridge introduced into America and hunted for sport – Northrop felt the name was appropriate for an aircraft that was going to be shot at throughout its service life.

This example was built in 1972 and TOC with RN. Serial number XW 999's service history is unknown to the author. SOC in 2008 and on static display at RAF Culdrose, in 2009 it made the 55-mile journey by road to CWM. Seen on 18 May 2024.

In March 1983 Piper Target Technology Ltd launched its prototype remotely controlled BTT – the Banshee. These craft had a top speed of 120 mph, remaining airborne for 1 hour 15 minutes. This example, serial number 3150, was built in 1999, a 400 series, and TOC with the British Army. It was one of twenty-six that were based at the Manorbier Ranges, all SOC in 2008 and put on display at Swansea Airport by Volunteer Glider Squadron. In 2010 it was stored in a hangar until 2013, when it was transferred to BDAC at Old Sarum. Pictured on 7 September 2024.

The RAE developed UAVs (Unmanned Aerial Vehicles). In the 1970s they developed gyro-stabilised remote-control craft using radar tracking that could be flown 'out of sight'. They carried 4.5-litre fuel tanks and could remain airborne for 90 minutes. This example, X-RAE 1, pictured at FAST on 7 September 2024, was built in 1976 and powered by specially developed electric motor and gearbox using lithium hydride batteries – conventional types were powered by internal combustion engines. The controls, gyro, radio, video camera and transmitter are contained within the nose section, powered by a separate cadmium-nickel power pack. The entire thing was catapult-launched under computer control.

The Short Brothers Stiletto SD.2 (the licence-built version of the Beechcraft AQM-37 Jayhawk) air-launched supersonic target drone. These were launched from an English Electric medium bomber Canberra jet, were powered by a liquid-fuelled rocket, had a top speed of Mach 4.0 (3,069 mph) and a range of 113 miles. This example was seen at FAST on 7 September 2024. Built in 1968 and TOC with RAF, it was used on the weapons range at RAF Aberporth.

Australian Government Aircraft Factories built the Jindivik radio-controlled target drones. Part of a bilateral agreement – the UK supplying the missiles and Australia the drones – the name 'Jindivik' comes from the Aboriginal word meaning 'the hunted one'. These craft used a three-wheeled jettisonable launching trolley for take-off and a retractable sprung skid for landing. This example, serial number ZJ 496, built in the early 1980s as MK104A type 700, TOC with RAF, took part in twenty-six recorded flights. SOC in 2003, it was donated to FAST. Pictured on its original launching trolley on 7 September 2024.

This Jindivik example, a MK103BL type 700, was built in the late 1970s and imported from Australia. TOC with RAF without an engine and some major components, and never allocated a serial number, it took part in nine recorded flights before crashing on 27 June 1995 and SOC. In 2001 the crashed fuselage was found at the bottom of a lake in Wales, recovered, and taken to CAAM. Seen on 20 April 2019 in an 'as found' condition. The tail fin is from a MK104AL type 700, serial number ZJ 489, which was scrapped in 2016.

Manufactured by Short Brothers during the mid-1980s/early 1990s, the Skeet aerial target system drone had a range of 6 miles under radio control and a top speed of 161 mph. This example, an Mk2 built in 1988 and TOC with the British Army, was used in gunnery practice on ranges in South Wales. Upon being SOC (year unknown to the author), it was donated to FAST. Pictured on 7 September 2024.

The Phoenix all-weather day and night real-time surveillance UAV was manufactured by BAE Systems. It had a top speed of 107 mph with a range of 415 miles. This example was built in 1984 and TOC with the Royal Artillery, until SOC during the early years of the twenty-first century. Donated to NMFS in East Fortune, it is pictured suspended from the ceiling on 20 October 2024.

The DJI Technology Co. Ltd introduced the 'Phantom' quadcopter UAV in 2013 – developed for domestic and commercial use in surveillance/reconnaissance. They had a top speed of a mere 34 mph with a meagre 3-mile range. This example, an FC40, was manufactured in 2014 for Syrian government forces, but captured by the Syrian Free Army in the city of Homs in November that year. Pictured on 20 October 2024 on display at NMFS.

General Atomics Aeronautical Systems manufactured MQ-1 Predator multi-purpose drones. These vehicles had a top speed of 135 mph and a range of 777 miles. Developed for reconnaissance use, later models were modified to carry two 108-lb anti-armour missiles. This example, an MQ-1B, one of the modified versions, was built in April 2005, TOC with USAF and serial number 03-3119. SOC in 2016, it had flown in 1,023 sorties and clocked up 17,050 hours (99 per cent during combat operations). Loaned to RAFH, it is seen on 5 January 2024.

In 1983 small British company ML Aviation produced a vertical take-off UAV – the Sprite – for use by the MoD. In 1988 following trials on board a USN Coast Guard cutter patrol vessel, the Swedish Army placed an order for 130; however, the company went into liquidation shortly after delivering a couple of craft. The MoD were still interested (along with a few countries) but no more craft were produced, leaving only a dozen or so ever built. This example, pictured on display on 7 September 2024 at BkAM, is the prototype example that was flown in 1983.

Chapter Ten

Experimental Craft

Air forces and military establishments have used various experimental aircraft over the decades. These craft have taken many forms, including engine testing, wing shape trials, supersonic technology evaluations and weapons testing, to name a few. With the advancement of technology in the twenty-first century, experimental aircraft continue to be used – although not on the same scale as during the Cold War.

Geoffrey Terence Roland Hill, aviator and aeronautical engineer, developed a series of tailless craft during the mid-1920s in an attempt to produce a safer form of aircraft. He named this the Pterodactyl (after the carnivorous flying reptile of about 150 million years ago). In 1925 he built Pterodactyl 1A in conjunction with Air Ministry, tested at RAE, launched as a glider and given serial number J8067. Seen at LSM suspended from the ceiling on 22 February 2020.

Serial number WG 774 was one of two built for Supersonic Research Aircraft by Fairey Aviation Co. in 1954. The Fairey Delta FD.2 were the first jets capable of doing 1,000 mph in level flight. This example, the first of the two, was extensively rebuilt by BAC (named BAC 221) in 1964 with the same original delta wing that was eventually used on Concorde. It is currently on display alongside the prototype at FAAM. Pictured on 16 December 2023.

A.V. Roe & Co. developed the Type 707 experimental jet designed to test the tailless thick delta wing configuration chosen for the new Type 698 Vulcan jet bomber, which was still undergoing development trials. Five were built and the first prototype made its maiden flight on 4 September 1949, but crashed on 30 September that same year, killing its pilot, and was scrapped. The Vulcan programme was completed and the prototype bomber was operational, but the four remaining 707s were still used as research aircraft.

This version, one of three survivors, serial number WZ 736 and built in 1953 as a 707A, remained in use with RAE until 1967. It was donated to MS&I (seen on 14 January 2012).

Manufactured in 1941 by Gloster Aircraft Co., the E.28/39 prototype was the first British turbojet-engined aircraft. Two prototypes were built, which could reach an altitude of 10,000 feet in 22 minutes (slow compared to the craft of the twenty-first century). They carried no armament, but had provision to carry two 0.303-inch Browning machine guns. The second prototype was built on 1 March 1943, but had a short existence – destroyed in a crash on 30 July whilst on a high-altitude test flight, an aileron stuck in position. The aileron is the small hinged part of the wings on an aircraft that controls the rolling or banking. The first prototype continued to be used on test flights until 1944, before going to the LSM in 1946. Seen on 22 February 2020.

SC.1s were two experimental fixed-wing VTOL aircraft – the first in Britain. They were built by Short Brothers in 1958 and used by RAE. These craft were powered by five Rolls-Royce turbojets – four used for the vertical flight and one for the horizontal – and had a top speed of 246 mph with a range of 150 miles. This example, serial number XG 905, was seen at UFT on 27 April 2011.

Built in 1954 by Rolls-Royce, earning the unflattering nickname of 'The Flying Bedstead', was this unusual craft, the Thrust Measuring Rig. A pioneering VTOL craft, it is 28 feet long and has the distinction of being the first jet-lift aircraft to fly anywhere in the world. This example, the first prototype built, is found on display at LSM on 22 February 2020.

This aircraft, seen on display at MAM on Christmas Eve 2023, is the one-off P.111, built in 1950 by Boulton Paul Aircraft and TOC with RAE. It was the first of many from different manufacturers designed to explore the characteristics of the tailless 'Delta Wing' configuration. It had a top speed of 649 mph and a climb rate of 9,000 feet per minute. SOC in 1958, following a period in storage, it was donated to the museum in 1962.

Serial number WK 935, a Gloster Meteor F8 fighter jet built in 1954 and TOC with RAF, was heavily modified to evaluate the effects of acceleration/inertia-induced forces whilst flying in a prone position – lying on your chest with your back facing upwards. It was tested in over 100 flights, clocking up 55 hours. The prone position concept was very feasible, but the introduction of 'G-Suits' made this prone pilot craft redundant. SOC after a year and put into storage, in 1965 it was donated to RAFC. Pictured on 23 December 2023.

Above left: During the 1970s Westland Helicopters launched the WG-25 project in order to develop a RPH (Remote-Piloted Helicopter) that could be used by the British Army for aerial surveillance work. The first built was the WR-05 MOTE in 1975. Made using model helicopter parts, it weighed 8 lb and was powered by two 1.4-hp model aircraft engines. Only one was built and it can be seen on display (along with the other three variants of the WG-25 project) at HCM as they were on 28 September 2023.

Above right: The second RPH built by Westland was the WR-06 WISP in 1976 – a scaled-up version of the 'MOTE'. It included a spheroid body to contain the engines and allow a 360-degree scan for the TV camera surveillance package. Three were built. They weighed 70 lb and were powered by two 5-hp two-stroke engines.

Westland continued with the WG-25 project and the next variant built was in 1978 – the WR-07 WIDEYE. This variant had an egg-shaped body, retractable undercarriage legs, a stabilised sensor package, weighed 275 lb and was powered by two 20-hp two-stroke engines.

The final variant of the WG-25 project was built in 1981 – the SHARPEYE. This one was actually allocated serial number ZS 782 – although never carried it in service. The body was more stealthy and aerodynamically built around the WIDEYE mechanical components. The entire WG-25 project was abandoned in 1983.

British Aerospace built a one-off technology demonstrator fighter – Experimental Aircraft Programme (EAP). With a maximum speed of Mach 2 (1,534 mph), it was designed to research the technologies later used in the Eurofighter Typhoon. First flown in August 1986, it flew in over 250 sorties until its final flight in May 1991 – fulfilling its intended purpose as a development aid.

In 1991 it was transported to Loughborough University. Its port wing was removed, providing a better view of the aerofoil cross section, and for two decades was used as an instructional aid to teach students. In March 2012, RAF requested that it be moved to RAFC following a rebuild and put on display in November 2013. Noted on 23 December 2023.

January 1954 saw the inaugural flight of the Fairey Jet Gyrodyne – a one-off experimental aircraft built by Fairey Aviation Co. This craft incorporated helicopter, gyrodyne and autogyro characteristics. TOC with the Ministry of Supply, serial number XD 759 (became XJ 389 due to duplication) was on a research contract aimed at gathering information/data for the follow-up Rotodyne project. Vastly underpowered, it could only carry sufficient fuel for 15 minutes of flight. SOC in 1961 and destined to be scrapped, it ended up as part of the RAFM collection. On display at RAFC until 1994, it then moved to BkAM. Pictured on 7 September 2024.

In 1930 Viennese-born Raoul Hafner, pioneer and engineer, built the experimental single-seat Hafner-Nagler RII Revoplane for the Austrian army. Powered by a 30-hp engine, testing began straight away. In 1931, it was rebuilt to replace the engine with a 45-hp rotary piston engine. In 1935 it was put into storage at Heston Aerodrome (not far from current Heathrow) and forgotten about. In 1961 it was discovered in a crate at Weston-super-Mare – how/when it got there remains a mystery. Refurbished by Westland apprentices, it was donated to the Shuttleworth Collection. Being short on space to display it, it was loaned to Torbay Aircraft Museum, where it remained until 1978. Raoul died in 1980 and ownership passed to his widow, who donated it to HCM. Seen on 28 September 2023.

The H.8 Rotachute one-man rotor kite was designed by Raoul Hafner with a top speed of 108 mph. Originally towed behind a Humber car, it was eventually towed by a Tiger Moth biplane. With a main rotor diameter of 15 feet, trials began in January 1942, continuing until late 1943, when the project was cancelled by the Air Ministry. This one, the fifth model (P-5) built in 1942 as a Mark III, was towed behind the Tiger Moth in June that year, on a 300-foot tow line, and released from the line at an altitude of 200 feet, making its first manned controlled flight. Further flights were made reaching altitudes of up to 3,900 feet. Seen on display at MAF on 17 August 2024.

The Raoul Hafner Rotabuggy – essentially a Willy's MB Jeep combined with a rotor kite – was intended to be developed as a way of air-dropping off-road vehicles behind or as near to enemy lines as feasible. This craft was 21 feet long with a main rotor diameter of 46 feet 8 inches and a top speed of 150 mph. During the first trial in November 1943 it was towed behind a Diamond 'T' truck – but the truck was not able to get enough speed to get the buggy airborne. The next trial saw a 4.5-litre Bentley Supercharged car used as a towing vehicle, and flights of 45 mph were achieved. The final trial occurred in September 1944 and the towing vehicle was an Armstrong-Whitworth Whitley bomber; this time the Rotabuggy flew for 10 minutes at 65 mph. With the introduction of vehicle-carrying cargo gliders, the Rotabuggy project was cancelled. The original buggy was scrapped during 1945/46, but MAF has this replica (seen on 17 August 2024) on display.

Chapter Eleven

Restoration

The vast majority of aircraft featured in this book all survive thanks to groups/organisations/museums who have worked very hard over the years rescuing many airframes from crash sites/wars, etc., and have painstakingly restored them to their former glory – not just as static exhibits, but to fully working flying craft again. They can often be seen taking part in various air shows throughout the country. The restoration process of many historical aircraft is an ongoing one thanks to those organisations whose aim is to preserve the past for future generations.

Above left: The Slingsby T.21B production version glider was built especially for RAF ATC. They were open cockpit, side-by-side, two-seater training gliders. This example (WB 969) was built in 1950, TOC with RAF, and SOC in October 1980 – it had been stored since August following a crash. RAF auctioned off their wooden gliders in the 1980s; WB 969 was sold to a gliding club in Wroot and re-registered as BGA.2036. Acquired by SYAM in 2001, on 30 August 2021 it was pictured as part of an ongoing complete restoration process.

Above right: Built in 1934 by Supermarine as a Walrus I, TOC with RAF and SOC in 1946, serial number W2718 was stored at Wroughton. Purchased by Somerton Airways of Cowes, it was given civilian registration G-RNLI. Sold in the mid-1960s, the fuselage was widened and used as a caravan (the owner had the hindsight not to throw any of the other parts away). It was as discovered in the 1980s and taken to the Hall of Aviation at Southampton. The full restoration process began. Due to space restrictions in 2018, it arrived at IWMD, and the restoration's progress was pictured on 23 September 2023.

With a top speed of 235 mph, armed with six Browning 0.303-inch machine guns, and able to carry a payload of 4,500 lb, the Vickers Wellington 1A was a pre-Second World War heavy bomber. This example, serial number N2980, was built in 1936 and TOC with RAF at Mildenhall. On New Year's Eve 1940, on a training flight over Scotland from RAF Lossiemouth, in a blizzard it developed engine trouble and was ditched in the icy waters of Loch Ness.

In 1976 it was discovered by a team of American Loch Ness monster hunters, and on 21 September 1985 was salvaged from the depths and found to be very well preserved, arriving at BAMM six days later. Seen on 29 May 2022, restoration work is ongoing. It can actually be said that this is at least one 'monster' that was found in Loch Ness and survives.

The Fairey Barracuda carrier-borne torpedo and dive bomber was the most widely used aircraft by RN during the Second World War. None of these craft remain intact, but in the 1970s FAAM began a project centred around the main fuselage and wreckage of a 1943-built MkII, and other salvaged crash site parts, in order to try and rebuild a non-flying composite example.

Serial number DP 872 was TOC with RNAS at East Haven, Arbroath. In August 1944, having left RNAS Maydown in Londonderry, 5 miles from the airfield it spun out of control and crashed into Blackhead Moss Bog, near Enagh Lough. The wreckage, recovered from the site in 1971, was taken to Yeovilton and stored. The project has permission from the MoD to gather parts from UK crash sites. Other Barracuda parts (to date) are from craft which crashed in 1945. During 2010 the recovered parts were on display for a short period at FAAM – in a representation of how the craft will hopefully look. Pictured on 18 July.

This Heinkel 162A-1 jet fighter was built in 1944 under the Emergency Fighter Program. It was armed with two 30-mm cannons, TOC with Luftwaffe and serial number 120235. Captured at Leck in Germany by Allied forces in 1945, it was transported by road to Farnborough and given serial number AM 68 RAF. Between 1946 and 1960 it was on display at RAF Cranwell, then transported to IWML, where it remained until January 2013. Transferred to IWMD, it is seen on 23 September 2023 undergoing a complete refurbishment to its former glory.

Douglas Aircraft Co. built Skyraider A-1 single-seat attack aircraft, which were used by USAF, USMC and USN. A top speed of 322 mph, they are armed with four 20-mm cannons and could also carry 10,500 lb of a combination of bombs, torpedoes, mine dispensers and unguided rockets. This 1950 example left the Douglas plant as an AD-4W, TOC with USN, serial number 124068. In 1953 it transferred to RN, serial number WV 106, redesignated as AEW-1, and SOC in 1964. Displayed at RNAS Culdrose until 1976, it moved to Flambards Holiday Village until 2000, then moved to Yeovilton and put into FAAM Cobham Hall's store. On 5 September 2019 it was pictured outside, surrounded by its parts, patiently waiting for its restoration to commence.

Piasecki Helicopter Corporation tandem rotor multi-mission military transport craft – the H-21 Shawnee/Workhorse. It had the capacity to carry twenty troops or twelve stretchers and a top speed of 127 mph with a 265-mile range. This 1957 example, TOC with the French Army, serial number FR41, was sent direct to Algiers in the Indo-Chinese conflict. Serving the French Army and Marines until SOC in 1968, it went to an army firing range near Toulouse, slowly decaying until rescued by Centre d'Etudes et de Loisirs Aerospatiaux in Grenoble. An attempted partial restoration was made, with the cockpit converted into a mini cinema. Due to downsizing it had to go. HCM, having a good relationship with them, added this example to their collection, which arrived in 2016. It is the only one out of 334 built that is preserved in the UK. These two pictures (taken on 28 September 2023) show the ongoing restoration of the cockpit and aft fuselage section. Sadly it is unlikely to be a complete restoration due to a shortage of certain parts.

Built in 1959 by A.V. Roe & Co., this Shackleton MR.3 marine patrol aircraft was TOC with RAF, serial number XF 708. In 1968 it was based in Northern Ireland and served at RAF Luqa in Malta between 1969 and 1972. SOC and taken to IWMD, in September 2014 it moved inside the museum's conservation hangar in need of much overdue restoration work. This 23 September 2023 picture shows the work progressing.

The McDonnell-Douglas F-4 Phantom II supersonic jet interceptor/fighter-bomber had a top speed of 1,470 mph (Mach 1.9) and a combat range of 420 miles. They could carry up to 18,650 lb of weaponry, comprising general purpose bombs, cluster bombs, laser-guided bombs, various missiles, etc. This 1963 example, a F-4-C-15-MC, TOC with USAF, serial number 63-7414, served for eighteen years, then transferred to Hawaii Air National Guard. It transferred in 1982 to New York Air National Guard. In 1986 it transferred to RAF Woodbridge for battle damage repair, SOC, and moved to the National Museum of USAF. In 1992 it was loaned to MAM partially dismantled. Pictured on Christmas Eve 2023.

Built in 1941 under licence by Fairchild Aircraft, this Bristol Bolingbroke IV maritime patrol/fighter was TOC with RCAF, serial number 9048, and SOC in 1946. It was sold to a farmer in Manitoba, who, despite using the cockpit as a hen house, intended to restore it – which never happened. In 1972 it was acquired by Military Aircraft Restoration Corporation but restoration was slow going, leaving there in 1976. It was stored at six different locations until 2006, then acquired by Aerospace Bristol, who stored it until it was moved into a conservation hangar in 2019. Pictured on 30 November 2024, showing progress being made on its restoration.

Bristol Aeroplane Co. built the type 170 Freighter Cargo aircraft. This example, built in 1953, TOC with Royal New Zealand Air Force and serial number NZ5911, was loaned during 1955 to Straits Air Freight Express cargo airline and given registration ZK-BJP. During 1975 it took part in the Vietnam War, used to deliver relief supplies and flying out refugees. SOC in 1977, it was sold to Dwen Airmotive in 1978 and used to ferry cargo between Ardmore and Whenuapai. Withdrawn in September 1979, it remained parked up at Ardmore until 2017, when it was purchased by Aerospace Bristol and shipped to the UK. Pictured during restoration in the conservation hangar on 30 November 2024. It's the only one of its type to be preserved in the UK.

Chapter Twelve

Gate Guardians

There are a few bases dotted across the country where retired military craft can be seen on display as static exhibits at the entrance to those installations. There are also craft displayed in a similar role with private companies, to add a touch of modern curio and which can act as a talking point, helping to promote their businesses by word of mouth without having the need to do much external advertising.

London Motor Museum (LMM) in Hayes opened its doors in 2012. Due to a dispute with the council over unpaid rates it closed in 2018. On 19 August 2016 this 1975-built Agusta-Bell AB-204B was the gate guardian. TOC with Italian Air Force, serial number MM 80279, it was allocated to Practica di Mare military airport in Lazio. In 1977 it was transferred to Frosinone, and after five years of service it was transferred to the Amendola Air Base until 2007 and SOC. Between then and 2013 it was on display at the Historical Museum of Communication in Rome. In January 2014 it was acquired by LMM.

With a top speed of 223 mph, the Sea Prince transport aircraft was manufactured by Percival Aircraft Ltd. Serial number WM 735, a T.1 built in 1953, was TOC with RN, serving until 1980 and SOC – its final allocation coming in 1976 at RNAS Culdrose as a navigational trainer. In 1981 it was owned by Atlantic & Caribbean Aviation Ltd and given civilian registration G-RACA, operating until 1995, when its civilian registration was cancelled. Moved to former RAF Long Marston Airfield, part of a small aircraft museum, on 22 June 2016, the museum appeared to be closed and the exhibits were left decaying and vandalised, as this picture at the airfield entrance clearly shows.

Transonic jet-powered fighter Hawker Hunter F.6 serial number XG 164 was built in 1956 and TOC with RAF, serving with West Raynham Station Flight. Transferred to FAA during the mid-1970s it was based at RNAS Brawdry. When the new decade had started it was transferred to RAF Halton, serial number 8681M, where it remained until 1995 and SOC. It was then put into storage at RAF Shawbury. In 1996 it was purchased by Military Aircraft Supplies Ltd and transported by road to their location in Higher Poole, Somerset. It is pictured at their main entrance on 16 March 1999. It was moved to CWM in 2014.

With a top speed of 440 mph, Jet Provost training aircraft were built by Percival/Hunting Aircraft Ltd. This 1959 example, serial number XM 358, was TOC with RAF. In 1989 it transferred to RAF Halton for ground instructional use, serial number 8987M. SOC in 1993, it was acquired by Witham Special Vehicles in Colsterworth. Sold and moved to North Scarle in early 1996, it was resold again and moved to Twyford in September that year. In February 2000 it was purchased by Newmead Farm, Newbridge-on-Wye, where it is the gate guardian for Quackers Indoor Play Centre. Noted there on 18 October 2021.

This Sea Harrier FRS.1 was built in March 1985 by BAe Systems. TOC with RN, serial number ZD 578, in September it transferred to RNAS Yeovilton, serving there for the next fifteen years, during which period it was converted to FA.2, then transferred in 2000 to HMS *Illustrious*. SOC in 2002, in December 2003 it became the gate guardian at the north side of RNAS Yeovilton. Seen on 16 December 2023.

In September 1980 this Lynx HAS.2 (serial number XZ 728) left Westland, TOC with RN. In 1981 it transferred to RNAS Yeovilton Naval Aircraft Support Unit, serving for sixteen years – converted to HMA.8 during this time. On 18 February 1997 disaster struck; whilst on board HMS *Monmouth* in stormy seas, preparing to take off, it broke free of its lashings, fell over the side and sank – the crew was rescued and the craft recovered later. Beyond repair, it was SOC and placed into storage. In 2007 it was placed as a gate guardian at RNAS Yeovilton. On 16 December 2023 it was placed outside HMS Heron Senior Officers' Mess Quarters.

Standing opposite the previous picture on 16 December 2023, this 1981-built Lynx AH.7 was TOC with RN and assigned to FAA at Yeovilton. Transferred to AAC, it served with them until SOC in 2013. It was then sent to Middle Wallop for spare parts removal in 2015. In October 2016 it arrived as a gate guardian at HMS Heron.

Built by BAe Systems in 1981, this Harrier GR.3, TOC with RAF, serial number XZ 987, was assigned to RAF Gutersloh – the nearest operational RAF base to the East/West Germany border. On 31 January 1992 it suffered a wheels-up landing at Belize International Airport in Ladyville, but was recovered and sent to RAF Wittering for repairs – although with withdrawal of Harriers from service fast approaching these were cancelled. Transferred to RAF Stafford in 1993, it was assigned serial number 9185M. After SOC, it was allocated to Beacon Barracks, west of Stafford, as a gate guardian. Pictured on 11 July 2024.

XP 745, built in 1964 by English Electric, was a Lightning F.3 interceptor fighter jet, TOC with RAF at Wattisham. Its last flight took place on 4 February 1975 at RAF Leconfield, becoming a spares source for the remaining fleet. In October 1976 with new serial number 8435M it transferred to RAF Boulmer and was on display until November 1992 and SOC. In April 1993 it was purchased by Vanguard Storage Ltd, dismantled, and taken to their warehouse in Greenford. It was kept under cover until restoration began in 2016. In 2019 it was at Weald Aviation for painting into 56 Squadron's chequered tailfin 'Firebird' colours (carried while serving with the squadron in 1965). Returned to Vanguard in September 2019, it was specially mounted within the purpose-built atrium at their Bristol headquarters. Pictured on 14 October 2023.

RAFC has two gate guardians; entering the site you are met by this 1956-built Hawker Hunter F.6 fighter-bomber/ground attack/reconnaissance jet. TOC with RAF, serial number XG 225, it served for thirty-two years before SOC. Transferred to RAFC, it has remained in position since then – serving in this role for three years longer than in active service when this 23 December 2023 picture was taken.

This impressive 1970-built Hawker-Siddeley Nimrod HS.801 Mk1 signals intelligence reconnaissance aircraft was TOC with RAF at Kinloss, serial number XV 249. In 1977 it transferred to RAF Luqa in Malta until 1981. In July 1981 it transferred to RAF St Mawgan and took part in the Falklands War as a reconnaissance craft. Post-Falklands it transferred back to Kinloss, and during 1983 it was converted to MR.2. In 1992 it was in storage at Kinloss; then in 1996 it transferred to RAF Waddington. In May 2011 it was in Cyprus for Operation Ellamy – the UK intervention in Libya. SOC in 2011, it went to Kemble for storage at Air Salvage International; it was dismantled, transported by road to RAFC, arriving in March 2012, reassembled and seen on 23 December 2023.

This Avro Vulcan B.2 bomber was built in 1963, TOC with RAF, serial number XM 607 at RAF Scrampton. In 1976 it transferred to RAF Waddington, and in 1979 it was part of the Supreme Allied Commander Europe. In 1981 it transferred to Brize Norton and took part in the 'Black Buck' bombing missions of the Falklands War, at Argentine-held Port Stanley Airfield – dropping a total of twenty-one 1,000-lb bombs, directly hitting the runway half a dozen times. Returning to England after the war, it continued to serve with RAF. SOC in December 1982, in 1983 it was a gate guardian at RAF Waddington, adjacent to the A15. Pictured on 14 October 2017.

The Middle Wallop base of Army Aviation Centre has four gate guardians – three on the right and one on the left of the approach drive. These pictures were taken on 17 August 2024.

First on the right is XZ 346, a 1978 Westland-built Aerospatiale Gazelle AH.1, TOC with AAC. SOC in 2004, it moved to RAF Shawbury for storage. It was a gate guardian at Neveravon Airfield in Fittleton, remaining there until 2014, when it moved to its current location.

Next is a 1966-built Westland Scout AH.1, TOC with AAC, serving with various squadrons. Serial number XT 638, SOC in 1998, was plinthed at this location.

The last of the trio was a 1978-built Westland Lynx AH.7 (serial number XZ 184), TOC with AAC and based in Detmold, Germany. Its squadron transferred in 1979 to Omagh, Northern Ireland, serving until 2014. It transferred to Middle Wallop and was SOC in 2015. It is plinthed where it is seen.

The craft on the left is a 1967-built Westland Sioux AH.1, TOC with AAC, serial number XT 827, and SOC in 1974. It went to the School of Electronic & Aeronautical Engineering at Arborfield, and was still there in 1990. Removed in 2010 to Middle Wallop, it carries the serial number XT 123.

In 1959 the French Army Light Aviation (FALA) were using 108 American-built Piasecki H-21 Shawnee/ Workhorse, 'Flying Banana' transport helicopters – so called because of the upward angle of the aft fuselage. Serial number FR60 was one of those. Built in 1957 and TOC with FALA, it served extensively in the Algerian War of Independence. SOC in 1998, it became a gate guardian outside a scrapyard in Villerperdue, France. Pictured there on 18 August 2007 looking in a sorry state. This is what the HCM example would look like if fully restored.